Thomas Wright

Churchwardens' Accounts of the Town of Ludlow, in Shropshire

From 1540 to the end of the reign of Queen Elizabeth

Thomas Wright

Churchwardens' Accounts of the Town of Ludlow, in Shropshire
From 1540 to the end of the reign of Queen Elizabeth

ISBN/EAN: 9783337324124

Printed in Europe, USA, Canada, Australia, Japan

Cover: Foto ©ninafisch / pixelio.de

More available books at **www.hansebooks.com**

CHURCHWARDENS' ACCOUNTS

OF

THE TOWN OF LUDLOW,

IN SHROPSHIRE,

FROM 1540 TO THE END OF THE REIGN OF QUEEN ELIZABETH.

EDITED, FROM THE ORIGINAL MANUSCRIPT,

BY THOMAS WRIGHT, M.A., F.S.A., HON. M.R.S.L., &c.

CORRESPONDING MEMBER OF THE IMPERIAL INSTITUTE OF FRANCE
(ACADÉMIE DES INSCRIPTIONS ET BELLES-LETTRES).

PRINTED FOR THE CAMDEN SOCIETY.

MDCCC.LXIX.

THE REV. EDWARD ff. CLAYTON, M.A.

RECTOR OF LUDLOW,

THIS LITTLE VOLUME IS DEDICATED

AS A TOKEN OF

VERY SINCERE RESPECT.

THE REV. EDWARD Æ. CLAYTON.

MY DEAR SIR,

      I am assured that in the noble Church of which you so worthily exercise the spiritual direction, or in anything which relates to it, no one can feel a greater interest than yourself. This church derived much of its importance from the Guild of Palmers, which seems to have exercised an authority over the building, that, with its other property, was transferred to the municipal corporation of the town. Thus, in the following records, any act of an extraordinary kind is usually done " by appointment of the Bailiffs." Hence, too, such of the papers relating to the former affairs of the church itself, as have been preserved, are mostly found in the municipal archives of the town. Among these, as you well know, is a large manuscript volume containing the churchwardens' accounts of Ludlow, from A.D. 1540, the thirty-second year of the reign of Henry VIII., to the close of the reign of Elizabeth. The greater part of these accounts I have printed in the present volume.

    The accounts open at a very eventful period. We are at the dawn of the Reformation. Four years before, two hundred of the lesser monasteries had been dissolved, and in the very year in which

our records commence the same fate fell upon the rest. During
the remainder of this reign we witness in Ludlow Church the full
exercise of the Romish service, with all its pomp and imagery;
and the first two years of the reign of Edward VI. seem to have
gone on much as usual; but the accounts of the two years which
follow are filled with details of the pulling down and sale of
images, and tabernacles, and other popish furniture. During Mary's
reign we can just trace the return to the old forms of worship; but
they are not brought forward forcibly to our attention, and it seems
as though our old townsmen hesitated, uncertain of the durability
of the new state of things, and unwilling to identify themselves with
it.   Then, during the reign of Elizabeth we can feel the tranquil
triumph of Protestantism, until, at its close, we approach another
age of troubles, destined to end in the temporary ascendancy of
Puritanism.

Such is a general view of the historical interest of these records.
In their more minute details we contemplate our church, and our
town, as they existed three centuries ago. These accounts show the
former, with most of its peculiarities, inside and outside; and the
continual labour and expense employed in repairing, mending,
whitewashing, adding to, is quite marvellous, so that the whole
revenue of the Corporation is commonly spoken of as receipts for
reparations.   The frequency of some of these is remarkable; such
as the mending of glass windows, the renewing and repairing of bells,
and the purchase of bell-ropes.   To judge from the wearing and
breaking of bells and ropes, we must conclude that the amount of
bell-ringing in Ludlow church during the sixteenth century was
almost unparalleled.   This, however, will admit of explanation.
Not only was Ludlow, in itself, an important town on the borders

of Wales, but it was the seat of a viceregal court, and no doubt whatever event caused excitement in the castle gave employment to the bells in the church.

In the same manner, some of the facts entered into these accounts, curious in themselves, reveal other facts no less interesting. Thus, the regular payment of a permanent officer employed to whip dogs out of the church—the dog-whipper—is remarkable as one of the almost forgotten characteristics of the olden time : but we are also led to conclude from it that the door of the church was in those times kept open daily during the whole day. I might point to other examples of this kind. It is not improbable that Ludlow Church had some customs and practices peculiar to itself. Among these, perhaps, were the regulations relating to the pews. It appears to have been the custom to grant to an individual a piece of ground measured out on the floor of the church, upon which he himself usually built his pew, which became his private property, and he could sell it, or leave it by will, or his heir inherited it. A part of the process of sale appears to have been a form of surrender of the pew to the parish. I have been told that this method of dealing with the pews has remained in Ludlow church down to a very recent period. We can hardly figure to ourselves the appearance the interior of the church must have presented, when the pews, separate from each other, of different forms and magnitudes, were scattered over it as described in the following accounts. The light thus thrown upon the early history of the pew system is very important, and I have ventured to repeat in an Appendix some remarks on this part of the subject which I had made on a former occasion in reference to our Ludlow records.

There is another point in which these accounts have a popular interest. They present us with the names of some of the leading

CHURCHWARDENS' ACCOUNTS

OF THE TOWN OF LUDLOW.

Reparacõns done by Richard Langforde and Willyam
Lacon, wardens of the pareshe churche off Ludlowe, anno Henrici octavi xxvij[to], anno Domini
1540.[1]

Item, payd unto Thomas Smyth for a barre of yryn weynge vj. li. and for the workemanshype of the same	ix d.
Item, payd unto Thomas Smythe for v. bordes to the same	vij d.
Item, payd to Thomas Kerver for closynge the wyndous in the westrie with the same bordes . . .	ix d.
Item, payd to master glasier for glassynge the wyndous in the vestrie	ij s. viij d.
Item, payd to the bellmon ffor yve and holye[2] at Chrystemas	ij d.
Item, payd for the holye candylle[3] . . .	ij s. vj d.

[1] Henry VIII. ascended the throne of England on the 22nd of April, 1509, so that his thirty-second year began on the 22nd of April, 1540. The clerk who made up these accounts must, therefore, have written *xxvij[to]* instead of *xxxj[d]*, in copying the account.

[2] The dressing of the churches at Christmas was a very ancient popular custom, and is often spoken of by the old writers. The ecclesiastical canons of the Western church, as far back as the seventh century, condemn it as a practice borrowed directly from the paganism of our primitive forefathers.

[3] This and the entries which follow refer to a custom which was observed with great solemnity in the Romish church at Easter. On Easter Eve they put out the old fires, and produced new fire from the flint, which was consecrated by the priest. People took home

CAMD. SOC.   B

Item, bought of m^r wardene for the pascalle, a dosen li. of

     bolene waxe, prysse . . . . . . vj s. viij d.

Item, payd for the makynge off the pascalle .   ij s. vj d.

Item, for woode and oyle to the same pascalle . .   iiij d.

Item, payd the belmon for his labor . . .   iiij d.

Item, spend on them when the hade made the pascalle   vj d.

Item, payd for our dynner the same tyme . . .   viij d.

Item, for wesshynge of autor[1] clothis and albes iij. tymes in

     the yeare, and the sowynge on of the valans of them, iij s. iiij d.

Item, payd to Richard Spone for brusshynge of the heygh

     autor . . . .   xij d.

Item, payd to John Loyde for the yryn that bereth the

     clothes afore the hygh autor . . . .   xij d.

Item, payd to Phillip Tynker and Mathow Buclermaker

     for drauyenge of the yryn and makynge of the stapuls   ij s.

Item, payd for coles to melt ledde for the same .   j d.

Item, payd for rynges and crule[2] and the sowynge on of

     them on the clothe that haungyth afore the heygh

     autor . . . .   iiij d.

Item, payd for lynyn clothe to pece owt the walans that

     hangyth over the heygh auter . .   vij d.

lights of this fire to renew the fires in their own houses, as carrying with it a sort of blessing to their homes (it was another relic of paganism). But chiefly they lighted from it an immense candle of wax, or taper, which was called the Paschal candle, and was consecrated with very great solemnity. This is told in the old Latin verses of Hospinian :—

> Cereus hinc ingens, Paschalis dictus, amœno
> Sacratur cantu ; cui ne mysteria desint,
> Thurea compingunt in facta foramina grana.

This was kept burning until Easter Day, when it was extinguished in the holy water, which was then renewed for the forthcoming year. The taper was generally very large, as will be seen by the entries in our churchwardens' accounts. In 1557, the Paschal taper for the abbey church of Westminster weighed three hundred pounds.

[1] *i. e.* altar.

[2] Crule, spelt in later times *crewel*, was a fine worsted thread, which was used of course for sewing on the rings.

Item, payd to Richard Spon for the peyntynge of the
valans [1] . . . . vj d.
Item, payd for a frynge that hangyt at the valans . xiiij d.
Item, payd to Richard a Pouelle for the pecynge of the
valans, and the souynge on of the frynge . . iij d.
Item, payd to Phelip Tynkere for the settynge up of the
valans . . . . vj d.
Item, payd to Philip Tynkere for mendynge the engle [2] ij d.
Item, payd to Thomas Hunt for mendynge of the crofer [3] for
ye sepulcre . . . . vj d.
Item, payd for borde nayle and lathe neale for the same
cofer [3] . . . . ij d.
Item, payd unto Croket for mendynge of a bare [4] for the
sepulcre . . . . ij d.
Item, payd for nayles, cordes, and pynys [5] to the sepulcre vj d.
Item, payd for rosene to make lyght and wyure [6] for the
clocke . . . . j d.
Item, payd to Thomas Hunt for mendynge on of the
clapurs . . . . j d.
Item, payd for whit ynele [7] yt John Chraulye had to make
gyrdyls . . . . j d.
Item, payd for cordes to hange the clothe and to draue the
clothe that hangyth in the mydes of the heygh chancelle in the Lent . . . . . . ij d.
Item, payd for ij. cordes to drawe up the clothe afore the
roode on Palme Sondaye . . . . . ij d.
Item, payd for rynges and crule and the souynge on of them
on the clothe on the mydys of the heygh chancelle iij d.

---

[1] The valance was the drapery raised over the high altar at the solemnity of Easter.

[2] There is in the MS. the mark over the *e* usually signifying the *n* to follow *e*; but, as this is sometimes used with no meaning in this Manuscript, I dare not resolve decidedly whether the word should be *egle* or *engle*.

[3] In the first of these examples the word is clearly written *crofer*, but probably the second is correct, *cofer*, in the sense of a chest. *ꝺ ꞓꞇ* .

[4] A bar. [5] Pins. [6] ? Wire. [7] A coarse kind of tape.

Item, payd to Cle for mendynge of the locke on the organ-
soler [1] dore . . . . ij d.

Item, payd for cordes for the bellys off the organs . ij d. ob.

Item, payd for mendynge of ij. keys, on for the great dore,
and the other for the wendynge dore [2] . . iiij d.

Item, payd to Moris Goodknappe for mendynge of a baudrycke [3] . . . . j d.

Item, payd to the organ bloere for his yeares wages . ij s. viij d.

Item, payd to the belmon for his yeares wages xvj d.

Item, payd hym for the coverynge of a pytt [4] . ij d.

Item, payd for mendynge of the parishe bere [5] . viij d.

Item, payd for neales for the same bere . . . ij d. ob.

Item, payd Philipe Tynkere for souder bestouuyd on the
churche at iij. tymes, xvij li., j li. d., iiij li. quarter, at
iij d. li. . . . . v s. ix d.

Item, payd for woode and colis and candels for the same busynes iiij d.

Item, for lyme and sande to the same . . . iij d.

Item, payd to a laborer for to pargytt [6] and helpe hym vij d.

Item, payd to William Poues, barber, for a rope for our
Ladye belle at xvj. fedome [7] . . . . xij d.

Item, bought a smalle roope at xxiiij e fedom for the fyrst
mase belle [8] . . . . iiij d.

Item, bought a roope for the cheymys [9] at xxx. fedome prys xvj d.

Item, payd for whyppynge of roopes . . . viij d.

Item, payd for whypcorde and lecure [10] for the same
roopes . . . . j d.

---

[1] The organ-soler was the floor on which the organ was raised.   [2] ? Winding-door.

[3] This was a part of the mechanism of the bell, often mentioned in old churchwardens'
accounts, the exact character of which is at present rather uncertain. Baldric, or baudric,
means a belt or girdle, and it is said to have been given to a belt or thong by which the
clapper of the bell was suspended.

[4] *Pit* seems to have meant a grave.

[5] The bier on which the dead were carried to their graves.

[6] To parget or rough-cast a wall.   [7] Fathoms.   [8] Mass bell.

[9] The chimes.   [10] Liquor.

Item, payd for colis [1] agaynst Chrystmas, Ester, Whytson-
tyd, and Alhalontyd,[2] to sense with and to weeche
the sepulere [3] . . . . iiij d.
Item, payd to master wardene for syngynge brede [4] . iij s. iiij d.
Item, payd to Philipe Tynker for brassynge of a kandyl-
stycke . . . . iiij d.
Item, payd for makynge clene of the leddes twys in the
yere . . . . viij d.
Item, payd to Lokear the smythe for reparacions of the
chymes . . . . xiiij s. iiij d.
Item, payd for lecer to lecur them withe . . . ij d.
Item, payd for v. lynckes fatt [5] of William Poues weynge
xij li. and iij. quarters, at ij d. ob. a pounde . ij s. viij d.
Item, payd for a lyncke fatt of Water Troytt weynge ij li.
at ij d. ob. . . . . v d.
Item, payd for makynge clene of the steple stayer . ij d.
Summa totalis, iij li. x s. j d.

Reseyttes of the churche the same yeare.

Reseyved at Ester . . . . . . xxxvij s. ix d.
Reseyved of mastere Foxe for m[r] wardens leystalle [6] . vj s. viij d.
Reseyved of ser Richard Bensone for his Lent leystalle vj s. viij d.
Reseyved of the good wyffe Benet for hyr husbandes ley-
stalle . . . . vj s. viij d.

---

[1] Coals, i. e. charcoal.   [2] All Saints.

[3] It was the custom to construct a sepulchre, of course representing that of the Saviour,
with various ceremonies ; on Good Friday, the hoste was placed in it, and men were paid
to watch it night and day until Easter day, in the morning of which the hoste was taken
out, and it was announced that Christ had arisen.

[4] The singing-bread was the consecrated wafers.

[5] Fat, in old records, means usually a vat, or vessel ; but it here signifies something
which was bought by the pound, probably fat for the links or torches.

[6] The meaning of the word *leystalle* or *laystalle* in connection with a church is not very
clear ; but it appears to have had some relation to a pew. One meaning attached to the
word is a place for cattle to rest in after a long journey.

Reseyved of Thomas Trevauns and Rouland Hunt for ser
    Rogers Huntes leystalle . . . . vj s. viij d.
Reseyved of Richard Hanlye for olde tymber . . iiij d.
        Summa ress. . iij li. iiij s. ix d.
And so the churche rest in ther dette . . . v s. iiij d.
Wherof the be deductide for wesshinge of the churche
    clothes . . . . iij s. iiij d.
And so the parishe ys indettede to them . . . ij s.

Die Lunæ, videlicet xvj° die mensis Februarii anno regni regis
Henrici octavi xxxj°, coram Johanne Taylor et Johan-
ne Lokyer ballivis domini regis villæ de Ludlow.

At whiche day it ys orderede and agreede be the seid baylifes
that the forseid Richarde Langforde ffrom hensfourth shalle pesably
have, occupie, and enjoye the pewe or sette in the churche late in
the tenure of Alice Lane decessede, ffor whiche pewe the seide bay-
lifes have awardede that the seide Richarde Langforde shalle content
and paye to the churche wardeyns, over the ij s. wherin the churche
upon hys account restith in hys debtt, the some of vj s. viij d. ster-
vinge,[1] whiche ys payde the seide day and yere etc. quinte.
                               ffinis.

The account of Wattare Taylor and Wyllyam Partrynge, beynge churche wardens, in the xxxij. yere of the rayne of kynge Henry the eight, anno Domini 1541.

Item, payde to master Langforde for a corde to hange the
    lawnterne in the body of the churche . . . iiij d.
Item, payde to Phelipe Jokes for the hangynge of the
    same . . . . ij d.
Item, payd for a corde to the sacrynge belle . . iiij d.
Item, payde for nayles and naylynge the bordes in the
    gallery . . . . ij d.

---

[1] The contraction is rather indistinct here, and the v apparently an error, for it is pro-
bably intended for sterling.

Item, payde for ij. handelles for the belles to Seasson .   ij d.

Item, payde to Seasson for mendynge the whole of y^e
secounde tenor . . . .   ij d.

Item, for a locke to the steple dore next the belles and a keye   v d.

Item, for another locke and key to the nether dore .   v d.

Item, for a locke and key to the nether dore of the ledes
over the churche porynche [1] . . .   v d.

Item, for a borde and the naylynge . . . .   iiij d. ob.

Item, for iij li. of candelles to the lawnterne in the body
of the churche . . . .   vij d. ob.

Item, for pavynge of a grave in saynt John chauncelle and
for lyme . . . .   iiij d.

Item, to Philipe Jokes for vij li. of sowder,[2] that he spende
on the sowthe syde of the churche . . .   xxj d.

Item, for his man and woode . . . . .   iij d.

Item, for a whype and belles . . . . .   vj d.

Item, for ij. mens laber ij. days and a halfe for castynge
downe snowe of the churche . . . .   xx d.

Item, for sopynge of the wallis withein the churche for ij.
men ij. dayes . . . .   xvj d.

Item, for a key to the wedynge dore [3] . . .   ij d.

Item, for the whypynge of the rope to the ffirst belle   iiij d.

Item, for mendynge of the pascalle borde [4] . . .   iiij d.

Item, payde for smale cordes to the sepullere . .   iiij d.

Item, for pessynge on of the pellers [5] of the sepullere   ij d.

Item, to Thomas Taylor for blowynge the organs . ij s. viij. d.

Item, for coles at Christmas and Ester . . .   ij d.

Item, for d li. of fraynkeinsence . . . .   ij d.

Item, for tackes and pyns to the sepulere and for whyte
ynkle to the awbes [5] . . . . .   iij d. ob.

---

[1] Probably it should be poryche, the porch.   [2] Solder.

[3] In a former passage, p. 4, the word is spelt distinctly *wendinge*.

[4] The paschal table.   [5] Piecing one of the pillars.

[6] For white tape for the albes.

Item, to John Shrawley for makynge of the alleyas[1] and
for paper . . . . iiij d. ob.
Item, for woode to make the pascalle . . . . ij d.
Item, spende on the barbers at the makynge of the pas-
calle . . . . xij d.
Item, for xiij. li. of waxe . . . . . vj s. vj d.
Item, payde for holy candelles . . . . ij s. vj d.
Item, payde to the belmon . . . . . xvj d.
Item, for oyle to the pascalle . . . . . ij d.
Item, for a roope to the secounde tenor . . . xvj d.
Item, for mendynge of the whele of our Lady belle . viij d.
Item, for mendynge the clapere of the secounde tenor . xij d.
Item, for mendynge the whele of the secounde belle . ij d.
Item, payde to the dekens for tendynge of the pascalle iiij d.
Item, for pessinge [2] of the gable roope of the chymes . iiij d.
Item, for a bawdryke and a yrone pynne to our Lady
belle . . . . ix d,
Item, for di. li. wyre to the chymes . . . . iij d.
Item, for mendynge of the chymes . . . . vj d.
Item, payde to master warden for syngynge brede . iij s. iiij d.
Item, to master warden for ij. surples for the ij
dekens . . . . iiij s. j d.
Item, to Phelipe Jokes for mendynge the pareshe crose xij d.
Item, to John Glassier for mendynge the wyndowe
over the gallery . . . . . . v s. viij d.
Item, for a barre of yron to Thomas Forten . . iiij d.
Item, for lyme to mende the churche walle . . xij d.
Item, to Phelip Jokes for ix li. of sothere [3] to mende the
ledes on the northe syde . . . . . ij s. iij d.
Item, for woode . . . . ij d.
Item, to Phelipe Jokes for his man for ij. dayes . . viij d.
Item, for mendynge one of the stopes of the great organs viij d.

---

[1] Perhaps for alios.   [2] Piecing.   [3] Solder.

Item, payde to Harpere for vj. dayes worke one the
 churche walles . . . . ij s.
Item, payde Tromper for caryenge of stonne and sande xvj d.
Item, to Roger Meysy for cuttynge downe of ellorns[1] in
 the ledes . . . . ij d.
Item, for mendynge the candlestycke one the hyghe altar ij d.
Item, for a lawntorne for the first mase . . . xiiij d.
Item, for ij. poundes of candles to the same . . iiij d.
Item payde m^r Alsope for makynge the bocke of the iiij.
 wardes . . . . viij d.
Item, for weyshynge [2] and sowynge the awbis . . ij s.
Item, to Thomas Seassone for a handle to the secounde
 belle . . . . ij d.
Item, for pessynge the rope to the fyrst belle . . ij d.
Item, to William Powis for a lynke and a cord [for] the
 great organs . . . . . vij d.
       Summa iij li. xxj d.

Receyttes.

Ressevyde of the olde churche wardens . . . xxiij d.
Ressevide at Ester . . . . . . xxxix s. ij d.
Ressevide of Watter Torites wyf for Annes Davis knel-
 ynge place . . . . xij d.
Ressevide of Thomas Heytone for the reversyoun of his
 fathers pewe . . . . vj d.
Ressevide by the bocke of the iiij. wardes . . xj s. ix d.
Ressevide a c. of irone lackynge x. pownde at . . vj s.
Ressevyde of Rycharde Rawlens wyf for Elsabeth Gwyns
 knelynge place . . . . viij d.
       Summa iij. li. xij d.
The pareshe restyth in oure dett . . x d.
    ffinis.

---

[1] Elder-trees.   [2] Washing and sewing the albs.

The acount of Larense Ffrenshe and John Draper,
beinge churche wardens, the xxxiij. yere of the
raine of kynge Henry the viij. anno Domini 1542.

Item, payde to Thomas Seasson for mendynge the chymes,
    and for wyre, and to nootes[1] to the barelle .   .   xiiij d.

Item, to Thomas Taylar for blowynge the organs   . ij s. viij d.

Item, for di. a li. of wyre for the chymes   .   .   iij d.

Item, for a locke for the steple dore .   .   .   .   iiij d.

Item, to mr Glasyer for a wyndowe in saynt Catorns[2]
    chaunselle .   .   .   . vj s. viij d.

Item, to Phelip Jookes for mendynge the cloocke and the
    weyche[3] .   .   .   .   iiij d.

Item, to Thomas Seasson for mendynge the chymes .   iiij d.

Item, to the barbere for the holly candelle .   .   . ij s. vj d.

Item, for a corde to blowe our Lady organs .   .   .   j d.

Item, to the pavier .   .   .   .   xvj d.

Item, to William Geyrse and his to mene for hayngynge[4]
    the belles in the steple .   .   .   .   xvj d.

Item, to Thomas Underwode for mendynge the irone
    cheyre in the heyghe quyre[5] .   .   .   .   vj d.

Item, to the smythe of Ludfortt for a new key to the
    churche dore .   .   .   .   .   .   iiij d.

Item, to Tromper for caryenge of x. cart loodes of ramelle[6]
    that was cast owt of the grate .   .   .   vj d.

Item, to John Pavier for his labor .   .   .   iij d.

Item, for pavinge before the grate .   .   .   j d.

Item, to Phelip Jookes for sother to the ledes .   . viij d.

Item, for fagootes ther .   .   .   .   .   i d.

---

[1] Notes?   [2] Catherine's.

[3] The Promptorium Parvulorum has "WECCHE, of a clokke," but gives no further explanation.

[4] His two men for hanging.   [5] The iron chair in the high choir.

[6] Rubbish thrown out of the grating.

Item, to Philip for xli. li. of lede, and the castynge of a
    new peise[1] for the clocke   .   .   .   .   .   ij s. ij d.
Item, to iiij. men that dide make clene within the churche
    walles   .   .   .   .   xx d.
Item, to Thomas Seasone for pessinge the belle ropes .   vij d.
Item, to John Crokett for irone to the stocke of the belle
    and the makynge   .   .   .   .   .   .   vj d.
Item, for iij. borthen of roodes to mend the loige [2] .   iij d.
Item, to Pyngle for iij. loodes of cley   .   .   .   vj d.
Item, to John Bube for iij. rynges of lyme [3]   .   .   vj d.
Item, to hym for lyme to whitt the wallis [4] .   .   .   j d.
Item, to John Mape for his labor iiij dayes .   .   .   xiiij d.
Item, to John Glasyer for settynge up the ij. paynes that
    were taken downe at m[r] Fullyardes buriynge   .   ij s. ij d.
Item, for vj. peces of tymbere to horse the belles [5]   .   iij d.
Item, payde Richard Sawyer for xiiij. li. of waxe for the
    pascalle   .   .   .   .   vij s.
Item, for the makynge of the pascalle   .   .   .   ij s. vj d.
Item, for oyle at the makynge of the pascalle   .   .   ij d.
Item, for pyns and tackes for the sepulcre .   .   .   ij d.
Item, for colis on Estere yeven [6] in the vestre   .   .   j d.
Item, to Thomas Season for pessynge of the bawdrycke for
    the chymes and mendynge the chymes   .   .   vj d.
Item, to hym for mendynge the boordes under the belles,
    and for iiij loitores [7] for the belle ropes   .   .   x d.
Item, for a pes of tembere to make the beme   .   .   xvj d.
Item, for the squarynge of hym in the woode   .   .   x d.
Item, to Rolande Huntt for the carege home   .   .   x d.
Item, to the kervers on the sayde beme for ix. dais worke   ix s.
Item, to Thomas Smythe for iij. bordes to the beme   vj d.
Item, for candles to the kervers   .   .   .   .   ij d.

---

[1] Weight ?   [2] Three loads , or bundles, of rods to mend the lodge?
[3] A measure of lime, but how much I cannot ascertain.   [4] To whitewash the walls.
[5] On which to suspend the bells.   [6] Easter Eve.   [7] I do not know this word.

Item, to Thomas Bolde for makynge the holes in the stone
    walle for the beme .   .   .   .   .   vj d.

Item, to m^r Langforde for vj. bordes to make the comyn
    pewis .   .   .   .   iij s.

Item, a pes of tymber to undersett the comyn pewis .   iiij d.

Item, to Hoper and his ij. men for the mendynge of the
    pewis iij. days and a d. .   .   .   .   . iij s. vij d.

Item, for nayles at John Seassons for the stiple [1] and the
    comyn pewis .   .   .   .   .   .   xij d.

Item, to Gregory Smythe for a new key to the loige [2] dore   ij d.

Item, to Philip Jookes for mendynge of the irone that the
    barelles of the chymes dothe goo in .   .   .   vj d.

Item, to William Powis for ij. belle ropes, on to the first
    belle, and anothere to the third belle .   .   . iij s. viij d.

Item, ij. lynkes at .   .   .   .   .   .   xvij d.

Item, iij. lynkes at .   .   .   .   .   .   xvj d.

Item, ij. lynkes at .   .   .   .   x d.

Item, vij. lynkes at .   .   .   .   .   . iij s. ij d.

Item, in cordes to draw the clothe before the highe alter in
    Lent, and for lynes to the sepulcre .   .   .   v d.

Item, Watter Troit, for one lynke .   .   .   .   ix d.

Item, to Richarde Sawier for iij. lynkes [3] .   .   .   xviij d.

Item, the barbers brekefast at the makynge the pascalle   viij d.

Item, for the alter clothis and towelles weyshynge thre
    tymes this yere .   .   .   .   .   .   xij d.

          Summa totalis .   . iij li. xvij s. ij d.

Receytes.

Item, receyvede at Ester .   .   .   .   . xxxviij s. iiij. d.

Item, of mistres Sellmon for a pytt .   .   . vj s. viij d.

Item, more of her for a pewe .   .   . iij s iiij d.

Item, of Davy Shermon for a pewe .   .   . iii s. iiij d.

---

[1] steeple.   [2] lodge.

[3] These links, or torches, were probably intended for lighting at the paschal fire.

Item, of John Scasson for ij. c. and iij. quarter and v. li. of
irone at . . . . xvj s. ix d.
Item, that my felowe hathe of Richarde Langfort for the
same pewe . . . . vj s viij d.
Item, that m^r Glassyer owithe . . . . vj s. viij d.

M^d. the pewe in varians betwen Thomas Cother and Richarde Langforde ys grauntede for the noble aboved speinde[1] to the saide
Richarde, as aperithe by an order made in thende of the accounte of the saide Richarde when he was churche warden,
made by John Taylore and John Lokyer, then baylifes.

Summa totalis of the receytes . iij li. xix s. ix d.

And so they reste indettede unto the churche of this yeres
accounte . . . . ij s. vij d.

flinis.

Memorandum, leide downe by the churche wardens,
Richarde Water and Moris Phillipes, as here after
folowithe, in anno xxxiiij° Henrici octavi, anno
Domini 1543.

In primis, a smale corde to holde up the sacrament over y^e
hye alter . . . . ij d.
Item, to Thomas Scasson mendynge of the first belrope iiij d.
Item, for a staple . . . . j d.
Item, paide to John Forten for ij. keyes, on to the quere
dore, and the other to oure Lady chappelle dore . iiij d.
Item, payde to Rogere Meysey for candles for the last
wynter . . . . viij d.
Item, payde John Gwyn for ij. bordes to make ye yates
in ye churchyorde . . . . . . xij d.
Item, payde to Kerie for ij. lasp[2] for the same yatt . iiij d.

[1] The noble above spent. A noble was 6s. 8d.   [2] latches.

Item, for a peyre of hynges to the same   .   .   iiij d.

Item, for nayles .   .   .   .   .   .   iiij d.

Item, to William Gers and his man for mendynge the secounde belle   .   .   .   .   .   .   xij d.

Item, to John Meredith for makynge the yatt   .   .   x d.

Item, for ij. hokes to hange the belle ropes   .   .   ij d.

Item, to sir William of Seynt Lenardes [1] for a pistille boke   xij d.

Item, for half a yarde of whyt fustian and for thryde [2] to
mende oure Lady vestmentes   .   .   .   .   v d.

Item, payde Thomas Taylor for blowynge the organs .   ij s.

Item, payde John Panyer for candles, evy, [3] and holle at
Christmas   .   .   .   .   .   .   iij d.

Item, payde for mendynge of the thride belle rope   .   iij d.

Item, to John Glasier for glasynge and mendynge the
churche wyndowes   .   .   .   .   .   .   xxij s.

Item, payde for ij. capias, on for Thomas Butlere, and the
othere for Sawier   .   .   .   .   .   vj d.

Item, payde to oure atturney   .   .   .   .   xij d.

Item, payde for a venire facias   .   .   .   .   xvj d.

Item, spent on oure xij. men [4]   .   .   .   .   xij d.

Item, payde John Russelle for iij. barres of iron to the
wyndow in the stiple   .   .   .   .   x d.

Item, payde Thomas Seasone for mendynge the chyme
gabulle rope and for lethere   .   .   .   .   viij d.

---

[1] " Sir William" was of course the priest of St. Leonard's, a little chapel on the northern side of Corve Street, Ludlow, the ruins of which were visible at no very remote period. Sir, the English representative of *dominus*, was the usual title of a priest. How it happened to the priest of St. Leonard's to sell a "Pistille Boke," or book of the Epistles, to the church of Ludlow, is not very clear. Perhaps he had employed his leisure in writing it, and sold the MS. to the churchwardens.

[2] Thread.

[3] Ivy. The decking of churches and houses at Christmas with ivy and holly is a custom of great antiquity, and is spoken against with strong disapproval by the earlier ecclesiastics, as being derived from the pagans.

[4] The jury, of course, in the course of a law-suit here alluded to. A penny a man for treating them seems moderate, according to our present notions.

Item, payde for a loke to set on the yatt . . . ij d.

Item, payde for makynge of the tryselle . . . ij s.

Item, payde for a corde to oure Ladye organs . . j d.

Item, payde for whesshynge of the churche gere . . viij d.

Item, for makynge of the pascalle . . . . ij s. vj d.

Item, payde for xiiij li. of waxe to make the pascalle . vij s.

Item, in expences at the makynge of the pascalle . xiiij d.

Item, payde towarde the lantern in the mydle of the
churche . . . . xviij d.

Item, payde to John Nycoles brusshynge of the hye alter iiij d.

Item, to m^r Staynere for wesshynge of the saide alter . ij s. iiij d.

Item, payde Thomas Pavyer for swepinge the churche xvj d.

Item, payde his sonne for whippynge doges [1] out of the
churche . . . . viij d.

Item, payde John Nycollas and his servaunt for parger-
ynge ande whitlymynge and swepynge the churche ij s. vj d.

Item, for lyme and sande to the same . . . xxj d.

Item, for nayles to the sepulcre . . . . . ij d.

Item, payde for pynnys to ser Richarde Cowper . ij d.

Item, for rynges to hange the clothe before the hye alter
and the mendynge of yt . . . . . iiij d.

Item, to Thomas Rushbury for mendynge the copes and
oure Lady vestement . . . . . . viij d.

Item, to Philip Jookes for settynge in a claper in the fyrst
mase belle . . . . xvj d.

Item, payde the sayde Philipes for sowder to the ledes and
for fyre . . . . xvij d.

Item, to m^r warden for ix. elles of dolas [2] and an half to
make ij. new albus . . . . . vij s. j d. ob.

---

[1] The dogs appear, in those days, to have been kept under little restraint, and to have
been very troublesome. From this necessity of driving them out of the church arose the
title of dog-whipper, which is still given in some parts of England to the church-beadle.
In the sixteenth century a similar title was given to the monk who had charge of the
church in some of the continental monasteries.

[2] Dowlas, a sort of coarse linen brought from Britany. —

Item, payde for iiij. elles of dolas to make Rusbiry a serples   iij s.

Item, for makynge the ij. albus and the serples [1] and mendynge of on albe .   .   .   .   xvj d.

Item, payde for iij. lynkes   .   .   .   .   ij s.

Item, for a corde to the first mas belle   .   .   iiij d.

Item, to John Ruselle for ij. stapulles to the mase belle   ij d.

Item, to Thomas Season pychynge and mendynge of the
first belle and the thyrde belle   .   .   .   viij d.

Item, payde m^r warden for the syngynge brede to serve
the churche for the whole yere .   .   . iij. s. iiij d.

Summa iij. li. iij s.

The Receites of Richarde Watier and Moris Phillipes, churche wardens, as here after folowithe.

Item, receyvede at Ester   .   .   .   xxxiiij s. viij d.

Item, receyvede of yerne [2] .   .   .   .   .   xxij d.

Item, receyvede of Alis Ffrences for her husbandes
lestalle   .   .   .   .   .   . vj s. viij d.

Item, receyvede of master Cox for his wyfes lestalle . vj s. viij d.

Item, receyvede of m^{rs} Glasyer for her pewe after the
disses [3] of her husbande .   .   .   .   xx d.

Item, receyvede of Richarde Watier for a pew after the
decesse of m^r Draper   .   .   .   .   xx d.

Item, receyvede for quarterage as dothe appere by ther
boke .   .   .   .   .   .   xxiij s. vj d.

Item, receyvede of ser John Vawer for peyntyd clothe   xvj d.

Item, receyvede of mastres Alsope for the revercon of
mastres Selman pewe .   .   .   .   .   [4]

Item, hyt ys grauntyde to Thomas Leawys that he and his
wyf shalle enjoye the half pewe in revercon after the
decease of master Hare, now in his possession, payinge   .   .   .   .   .   ij s.

---

[1] surplice.   [2] *i.e.* for iron—old iron from the church repairs.

[3] decease.   [4] The sum is not entered.

Item, hyt ys grauntede to Richarde Waties half of the pewe
 whiche Thomas Leawys hath in possession, payinge xx d.
    Sum rec. . . iij. li. xviij s. iiij d.
    Sum pd. . . iiij li. iij s.
 And so the parishe restythe in the
  churche wardens dett . iiij s. viij d.
           ffinis.

The accountes of Robert Adder and Richarde Lane,
 churche wardens in the yere of the rayne of kynge
 Henry the eight xxxv., anno Domini 1544.

Item, payde to Thomas Yevans for blowynge the organs ij s. viij d.
Item, for a li. of candles to the prest for to synge the fyrst
 mase . . . . j d. ob.
Item, d. a li. of wyer . . . . . . iij d.
Item, payde John Torner for ij. peces of tember to make
 the gratt [1] . . . . . . iiij d.
Item, to William Gers for iij. dayes worke . . xviij d.
Item, to William Swese for iij. dayes worke . . xv d.
Item, to John Yerenmonger for iij. dayes worke . xv d.
Item, to William Geres for a pece of tymber . . ij d.
Item, iiij. poundes of candles to the fyrst mase . . vj d.
Item, to Richarde Lane for ij. peces of tymber for the
 grate . . . . xvj d.
Item, to John Season for a belle-rope for the first belle ij s.
Item, for the same belle a bawrycke . . . . vij d.
Item, a corde to the first mas belle . . . . j d.
Item, payde for pessynge of a belle-rope . . ij d.
Item, for pesynge of the whele of the seconde tenor . x d.
Item, for a corde to the organs . . . . j d.
Item, for a bawdrike to the seconde tenor . . vij d.

---

[1] Grate, or trellis. The Promptorium Parvulorum has, " GRATE, or trelys wyndowe,
Cancellus." The cross-bars of the window were usually of wood.

Item, payde for iiij. elles of dolas to make Rusbiry a serples   iij s.
Item, for makynge the ij. albus and the serples [1] and men-
    dynge of on albe . . . . xvj d.
Item, payde for iij. lynkes . . . . . . ij s.
Item, for a corde to the first mas belle . . . iiij d.
Item, to John Ruselle for ij. stapulles to the mase belle   ij d.
Item, to Thomas Season pychynge and mendynge of the
    first belle and the thyrde belle . . . . viij d.
Item, payde mr warden for the syngynge brede to serve
    the churche for the whole yere . . . . iij. s. iiij d.
                    Summa iij. li. iij s.

The Receites of Richarde Watier and Moris Phillipes, churche wardens, as here after folowithe.

Item, receyvede at Ester . . . . . xxxiiij s. viij d.
Item, receyvede of yerne [2] . . . . . . xxij d.
Item, receyvede of Alis Ffrences for her husbandes
    lestalle . . . . vj s. viij d.
Item, receyvede of master Cox for his wyfes lestalle . vj s. viij d.
Item, receyvede of mrs Glasyer for her pewe after the
    disses [3] of her husbande . . . . . xx d.
Item, receyvede of Richarde Watier for a pew after the
    decesse of mr Draper . . . . . xx d.
Item, receyvede for quarterage as dothe appere by ther
    boke . . . . xxiij s. vj d.
Item, receyvede of ser John Vawer for peyntyd clothe   xvj d.
Item, receyvede of mastres Alsope for the revercon of
    mastres Selman pewe . . . . . . [4]
Item, hyt ys grauntyde to Thomas Leawys that he and his
    wyf shalle enjoye the half pewe in revercon after the
    decease of master Hare, now in his possession, pay-
    inge . . . . ij s.

----

[1] surplice.   [2] i. e. for iron—old iron from the church repairs.
[3] decease.   [4] The sum is not entered.

Item, hyt ys grauntede to Richarde Waties half of the pewe
    whiche Thomas Leawys hath in possession, payinge   xx d.
         Sum rec.   .   .   iij. li. xviij s. iiij d.
         Sum pd.   .   .   iiij li. iij s.
    And so the parishe restythe in the
      churche wardens dett   .   iiij s. viij d.
                               flinis.

The accountes of Robert Adder and Richarde Lane,
churche wardens in the yere of the rayne of kynge
Henry the eight xxxv., anno Domini 1544.

Item, payde to Thomas Yevans for blowynge the organs   ij s. viij d.
Item, for a li. of candles to the prest for to synge the fyrst
    mase .   .   .   .   j d. ob.
Item, d. a li. of wyer   .   .   .   .   .   .   iij d.
Item, payde John Torner for ij. peces of tember to make
    the gratt [1]   .   .   .   .   .   .   iiij d.
Item, to William Gers for iij. dayes worke   .   .   xviij d.
Item, to William Swese for iij. dayes worke   .   .   xv d.
Item, to John Yerenmonger for iij. dayes worke   .   xv d.
Item, to William Geres for a pece of tymber   .   .   ij d.
Item, iiij. poundes of candles to the fyrst mase   .   .   vj d.
Item, to Richarde Lane for ij. peces of tymber for the
    grate   .   .   .   .   xvj d.
Item, to John Season for a belle-rope for the first belle   ij s.
Item, for the same belle a bawryeke   .   .   .   vij d.
Item, a corde to the first mas belle   .   .   .   j d.
Item, payde for pessynge of a belle-rope   .   .   ij d.
Item, for pesynge of the whele of the seconde tenor   .   x d.
Item, for a corde to the organs   .   .   .   .   j d.
Item, for a bawdrike to the seconde tenor   .   .   vij d.

---

[1] Grate, or trellis. The Promptorium Parvulorum has, "GRATE, or trelys wyndowe,
Cancellus." The cross-bars of the window were usually of wood.

Item, for the holly candelle . . . . . ij s. vj d.

Item, for ij. lynkes to William Powis . . . xij d.

Item, for mendynge the cobort [1] at the hyghe alters ende ij d.

Item, for mendynge the while of the secounde tenor . iiij d.

Item, for ij. cordes to draw the clothe in Lent in yᵉ hye
quyre . . . . iiij d.

Item, to Thomas Season for mendynge the cope for Lent x d.

Item, to Yowan Troyte for a lynke . . . . vij d.

Item, for a key to the loyge dore . . . . ij d.

Item, for oyle to the makynge of the paschalle . . ij d.

Item, spende on the barber at the makynge of the paschalle xij d.

Item, to William Gers and his man for makynge of the house
over the grate . . . . xxij d.

Item, for bordes to the same house . . . . xiiij d.

Item, for nayles . . . . ij d.

Item, to the pavier . . . . xvj d.

Item, for nayles and pyns to the sepullere . . . ij d. ob.

Item, for frankencence . . . . . . j d.

Item, for weshynge the churche gere . . . viij d.

Item, for tendynge the paschalle . . . . iiij d.

Item, to Thomas Season for mendynge the gable and the
chymes . . . . viij d.

Item, for a yende of a rope to the secounde belle . iiij d.

Item, for mendynge the churche dore key . . . j d.

Item, to them that brought the churche lader out of the
castelle . . . . ij d.

Item, for xij. li. of waxe for the paschalle . . . viij s.

Item, to Yowan Troyte for a belle-rope . . . xij d.

Item, to mʳ glasyer for a glassynge borde [2] . xvj d.

Item, for mendynge ij. banner clothes . . . ij d.

Item, for a pece of a rope to the chymes . . . v d.

---

[1] Cupboard.

[2] It would appear that, when the glazier came to work, a table (board) was made for him at the expense of the churchwardens.

Item, to Thomas Season for pesynge the same rope and
the belle-ropis . . . . vj d.
Item, for rossen[1] to the glasyer . . . . . j d.
Item, to the glassyer for a fortnyghtes worke in saynt
Margeretes chapelle and on the southe ylle of the
steple . . . . iiij s. viij d.
Item, for iiij li. of soder . . . . . xx d.
Item, for xx li. of cast lede . . . . . xx d.
Item, to William Marten for fastenynge the glassen wyn-
dos in the body of the churche . . . . iiij d.
Item, to Thomas Cocke, for helpynge the glasyer di. a day ij d.
Item, to the glasyer for xx. li. of lede . . . xx d.
Item, ij. li. of soder . . . . . . vij d.
Item, for glace to the steple . . . . . xvj d.
Item, to Thomas Cocke, a days worke . . . iiij d.
Item, for helpynge to remove the lader in the gallerie iij d.
Item, to the glassyer for v. wekes worke and di. . v. s. x d.
Item, a belle-rope to the fyrst belle . . . . ij s.
Item, for makynge of the pascalle . . . . ij s. vj d.
Item, for a lynke . . . . vj d.
Item, to Jowan Troyte for a lynke . . . . vj d.
Item, for the glassiers borde for v. wikes and a di. . vij s. iiij d.
Summa, iij. li. x s. viij. d.
Item, more for costes as apperith on the other syde . iiij d.
Summa, iij li. xj s.

Resseytes.

Item, receyvede at Ester . . . . . xxix s. iiij d.
Item, receyvede of William Partryge yonger for halfe a
pewe and for the reversyon after Hasylwoodes . ij s. iiij d.
Item, receyvede for the olde tymber that was on the grate vj d.
Item, of the iiij. wardes . . . . . . viij s. xj d.

---

[1] Resin.

Item, of m^r Shermon for his close in Galfforde [1] .   .   viij s.
Item, we have to receyve for John Tornors and his
  wyfes grave   .   .   .   . xiij s. iiij d.
Item, of mestres Glasser   .   .   .   .   .   . vj s. viij d.
          Summa iij. li. ix s. j d.
The whole charges of the reparacyons withe alle costes   iij li. xj s.
Summa of ther resceyttes amountythe   .   .   . iij. li. ix s. j d.
And so the pareshe remaynithe in dett   .   .   .   xxiij d.
  wiche they have remyttede, and so quytt.
This accompt was taken before m^r Foxe and Richard Langforde, the
  baylys of the seide towne, Thomas Wheler, Thomas Cother,
  John Hulke, and others, the vth day of November.
          ffinis.

Costes and charges doon by me Holle ap Rees and John
    Clee, churche wardens of Ludlow, in the tyme of
    m^r William Fox and Richart Langfort, then beynge
    baylifes of the towne of Ludlow, anno Henrici
    octavi.
          Anno Domini 1545.

In primis, payde for ij. candlestickes that were broken   x d.
Item, to Thomas Jevance for Alhallon quarter for blow-
  ynge the organs   .   .   .   .   .   .   viij d.
Item, payde for vij. li. of candles   .   .   .   .   x d. ob.
Item, for wyer to the clocke   .   .   .   .   ij d.
Item, to the belmon for makynge clene of the churche   iiij d.

---

[1] I have not been able to trace any property in Galford belonging to the church bearing,
as we might expect, such a name as Shermon's Close; but it is very singular that there is
a court in Galford, on the left-hand side going towards Cainham, which is called Charmer's Court, but which is understood to have derived its name from an old man named, or
nicknamed, Dickey Charmer, who went about the town selling fish, &c. and was well
known some years ago, and who lived in this court. May not the two names have been
confounded, and the name of the Charmer of modern Ludlow have replaced the Shermon
of these Churchwarden's Accounts? It is a sort of transformation which is met with not
uncommonly in our old towns.

Item, payde for reddynge [1] the churche of stonys . ij d.

Item, payd for mendynge of our Lady belrope . ij d.

Item, payde for a loke to the clocke dore . . . vij d.

Item, payde to Johan Troyte widow for ij. lynkes and for
candels to make holye candels . . . . . ij s. iiij d.

Item, for mendynge of the vestrie wyndow and for makynge clene of the ledes . . . . . xiij d.

Item, for a bawdrik to the first belle clapur . . iij d.

Item, for a corde that dyd drawe the clothe in the heye
quere . . . . iij d.

Item, for oyle to the pascalle . . . . . ij d.

Item, for waxe to the pascalle . . . . iiij s.

Item, spende at the makynge of the pascalle . . vj d.

Item, payde for makynge of the pascalle . . . xv d.

Item, to the blower of the organs for candlemas quarter viij d.

Item, payde for rossen . . . . . . j d.

Item, for pynnees and sope . . . . . ij d.

Item, for a corde to the organs . . . . . j d.

Item, for wyer and nayles to mende the chymes . vij d.

Item, for settynge the albus to every vestment . x d.

Item, to ser Richarde Cupper in a reward a peir of gloves
price . . . . ij d.

Item, payde for colles . . . . . . j d.

Item, payde for a lynke . . . . . . xiiij d.

Item, payde to the servers of wyne on Easter day . ij d.

Item, for settynge up of a loker to drawe the corde before
the crucifixe . . . . j d.

Item, for xij li. of sowder to mende the ledes . . xviij d.

Item, to his servaunt for his wages . . . ij d.

Item, for a bawdrek to the secounde tenor . . . x d.

Item, payde for a while [2] to the secounde tenor . . xx d.

Item, for settynge up of the while . . . . xiij d.

Item, for mendynge the secounde belle-rope . . ij d.

---

[1] Ridding, clearing.   [2] A wheel.

Item, for a canapye on Corpus Xp̄i day . . . ij d.
Item, for nayles and pynnes to the canapye . ij d.
Item, payde for iiij. belropes . . . . . v s.
Item, for a borde and nayles and for mendynge of a dore
goynge up to the clerkes chamber . . viij d.
Item, payde to Troyte wyfe for a lynke . . . viij d.
Item, payde for lyme . . . . . . v d.
Item, for takynge downe the beame in the middle of the
churche . . . . x d.
Item, payde to the pavior . . . . . iiij d.
Item, payde for candles . . . . . . ij d.
Item, for mendynge of the wyndow in saynt Margretes
chauncelle and for pargettynge the leades to Thomas
Season . . . . iiij s. viij d.
Item, payde to Johan Troyte for a lynke . . . viij d.
To oure clerke for the yere . . . . . xij d.
Item, payde for a sitacon ¹ . . . . . vj d.
Item, to Thomas Season for sowder and for mendynge of
the leedes . . . . vj d.
Item, for makynge clene of the glassen wyndowes . j d.
Item, payde for candles . . . . . . iij d.
Item, payde to sir William Wyatt for correkynge of alle
burialles and christynynges for the yere . . iiij d.
Summa . . xxiij s.
Summa totalis Holle ap Rees, iij li. iij s. j d. ob.

Receyttes.

In primis, receyvede of the Easter boke my parte . xvj s.
Item, receyvede of mr Cothere for the pewe anent the fonte
my parte . . . . ˙ xx d.
Item, receyvede of mrs Poton in parte of payment of vj s.
viij d. for the pewe under the pilpitt and the rest to
be payde . . . . v s.

_____
¹ A citation, or summons.

at the feast of the nativitie of saynt John Baptiste then
next ensuynge.

Item, receyvede of Elizabeth Glover for her knelynge place
behynde the northe churche dore   .   .   .   viij d.

John Clees part.

In primis, payde for a key to the dore that goothe up into
the stiple . . . .   ij d.

Item, for makynge of the bow of the keye of the churche dore   j d.

Item, payde for mendynge of the payne of glase in the
stiple on the southe syde to Thomas Season   .   xiij d.

Item, payde for makynge of the churche boke to Richarde
Tomlyns   .   .   .   .   viij d.

Item, to the belmon his quarterrage   .   .   .   .   ij d.

Item, payde for colles   .   .   .   .   .   .   j d.

Item, for mendynge of the locke of the lodge dore and a
key   .   .   .   .   iij d.

Item, payde for a key to the dore at the hede of the dekyn
chamber,[1] and to the chamber dore a key   .   .   iij d.

Item, payde to William Powis for a lynke   .   .   viij d.

Item, for mendynge of the glasse in the grett wyndow   iiij d.

Item, payde to Thomas Season for mendynge of the vestrie
wyndow and makynge clene of the leedes   .   .   xiij d

Item, to William Powis for candles at Christmas   .   xiiij d.

Item, payde to Phillip Jookes for j. li. of sowder to mende
the leedes . . . .   iij d.

Item, for mendynge of the belle-rope to John Taylor .   ij d.

Item, for a sheme[2] of wode at the makynge of the pascalle   ij d.

Item, spende at that tyme   .   .   .   .   .   v d.

Item, payde for wax to the pascalle my parte   .   .   iiij s.

Item, for nayles and tackes to the sepulcre .   .   .   ij d.

Item, for settynge of the clothe to the churche dore   .   j d.

---

[1] The Deacon's chamber.   [2] A seam or horse-load of wood.

Item, payde for pynnes and whipcorde   .   j d.
Item, payde for coles   .   .   .   .   j d.
Item, payde for xij. li. of sowder to the leedes .   .   xviij d.
Item, for his servaunt wages [1]   .   .   .   .   ij d.
Item, for mendynge of our Lady belrope and the loker   iij d.
Item, payde for a while [2] to the first belle my parte .   xx d.
Item, payde for makynge of the pascalle my parte   .   xv d.
Item, for mendynge of the chymes to John Forten   .   xiiij d.
Item, for mendynge of the stocke of the first belle and for
     nayles   .   .   .   .   viij d.
Item, payde for the mendynge of the first and secounde
     belropes   .   .   .   .   iiij d.
Item, to the blower of our organs for half a yere   .   xvj d.
Item, payde for mendynge of the berre [3]   .   .   .   vj d.
Item, payde for mendynge of iij. cantylcopes [4]   .   .   iij d.
Item, payde to Gers for mendynge the arche   .   .   xij d.
Item, payde for candelles   .   .   .   .   .   j d.
To our clarke for the yere my parte   .   .   .   xij d.
Item, payde for a sitacon [5] my parte .   .   .   vj d.
Item, payde for clothe to make an albe   .   ˙   .   iiijd.

Summa,   .   xxij s. iiij d.

Memorandum, that I John Clee have receyvede for the
use of the churche as here after folowith.

In primis, receyvede of the Easter boke my parte   .   xvj s.
Item, receyvede of m[rs] Cother for her pewe my parte .   xx d.
Item, receyvede for m[r] Harez pytt   .   .   .   .   vj s. viij d.

Summa   .   xxiiij s. iiij d.

And so the seyde churche wardeyn restithe in
dett to the churche for his parte   .   vij s.

which is payde and so quite.

Summa totalis   .   iij li. v s. iij d.

flinis.

---

[1] The writer has apparently omitted the name of this servant's master.   [2] A wheel.
[3] The parish bier.   [4] I cannot explain satisfactorily this word.   [5] For a citation.

John Belle and William Clonton churche wardens of Ludlow anno Edwardi sexti primo, viz. the xvj. day of November, &c.

Anno Domini 1546.

In primis, payde for syngyng brede at dyverse tymes   ij s. viij d.

Item, payde to Hew Watson, for a bawdrike to the first belle . . . . x d.

Item, for mendynge of our Lady belle whele . . iiij d.

Item, payde for xvj. li. of candeles . . . . iij s. ij d·

Item, for makynge clene over the hye alter the imagery worke at Christmas . . . . . . xij d.

Item, payde for shotynge of the gable¹ to the chymes . iiij d.

Item, for thonges to the sayde gable . . . j d.

Item, for wyer and the mendynge of the chymes viij d.

Item, payde for mendynge of the crosse staffe . ij d.

Item, payde for canysˣ to sett candelles in . . ij d.

Item, for shuttynge of the smalle rope to the chymes . ij d.

Item, for mendynge of ij. hammers,³ a stapulle, and a sprynge, and the settynge on of them . . xvj d.

Item, payde for coverynge of mʳ Whittalles grave . iiij d.

Item, payde for colles . . . . . ij d.

Item, for an hammer to the chymes . . . . ij d.

Item, payde for makynge ij. serples . . . . viij d.

Item, for clothe to make ij. serples for the decons . iiij s. viij d.

Item, for iiij. lokers to the belles . . . . viij d.

Item, payde for a hande to the for belle . . . ij d.

Item, for shotynge and pychynge the secounde tenour rope iiij d.

Item, for pynnes and borde nayles . . . j d. ob.

---

¹ The cable.   ² cans.

³ The hammers were for the chimes.

Item, payde for mendynge of the belles and ropes ryng-
     ynge at kynges Harry dirge [1] . . . .   iiij d.
Item, payde for ij. stapulles to the new hande . .   j d.
Item, for haspes and ij. stapulles to our Lady chapelle dore   ij d.
Item, payde for hangynge the clothe before the rode .   ij d.
Item, for a locke and a key to the dore goynge to the belles   vj d.
Item, payde for a trisselle and holy candelles . . ij s. vj d.
Item, for a loker, and pesynge of the for belle rope   iiij d.
Item, payde for tackes . . . . . .   j d.
Item, for mendynge the secounde tenor while . .   ij d.
Item, payde for ij. girdelles . . . . .   ij d.
Item, payde for ynkille [2] to make streynges to the amyas [3]   j d.
Item, for piche and thonges to mende the chymes gable   j d.
Item, for shotynge on hammer and a sprynge . .   j d.
Item, payde to William Gers and his man for a day and a
     half for hangynge the belles whiche were out of the
     stocke . . . .   xvij d.
Item, payd for mendynge the parich bere . . .   iiij d.
Item, to Season for mendynge the chymes and for cuttynge
     downe the ellors and weedes about the churche .   vj d.
Item, payde to Rushbiri man for pysinge [4] of a rope   ij d.
Item, for xij. li. of sowder and the workynge of ytt upon
     the sothe ile of the churche . . . .   v s.
Item, payde for cole and woode . . . .   ij d.
Item, for the hire of a horse to fache [5] the rope for the
     chymes . . . .   viij d.
Item, for stele to a hammer, and a sprynge to the chymes   ij d.
Item, payde for a gable . . . . . .   viij s.
Item, payde for a rope to the secounde tenor . .   xiiij d.
Item, to Thomas Season for a dais worke of the belle whiles   vj d.

---

[1] The dirge celebrated on the death of King Henry VIII. The King died on the morning of Friday, January 28th, 1547.
[2] Tape. See before, p. 7.   [3] amice.   [4] piecing.   [5] fetch.

Item, payde for coverynge m^{is} Rogers grave   .   ij d.

Item, payde for wax to the pascalle   .   .   ix s. iiij d.

Item, payde Thomas Taylor for blowynge the organs   ij s. viij d.

Item, payde to Halle   .   .   .   .   .   ij s. viij d.

Item, payde for a rope to the first belle   .   .   xiij d.

Item, for nayles and tackes to the sepulcre   .   ij d.

Item, payde for colles   .   .   .   j d.

Item, payde for oyle and woode   .   .   iiij d.

Item, payde for our brekfastes   .   .   .   xij d

Item, payde for a rope to the secounde belle   .   .   xiij d.

Item, to Thomas Season for mendynge of the chymes and

    shotynge of the gable   .   .   .   .   v d.

Item, payde to the decons for tendynge the Easter tapur   iiij d.

Item, to Rushbiry for mendynge of a cantilcop   .   v d.

Item, payde to Stephyn Knyght for nayles   .   .   iiij d.

Item, payde for coverynge of my lady Tounsende mother

    grave and Alis Bonnettes grave   .   .   .   iiij d.

Item, payde to ser Richarde Copper for the cannoppy   x d.

Item, payde to the vycyter servauntes   .   .   xiiij d.

Item, for a rope to the first mas belle   .   .   vj d.

Item, to Season for mendynge the chymes   .   .   iij d.

Item, payde to Crosse for mendynge of an hammer   .   ij d.

Item, to Hew Watson for mendynge of the bawdrike to

    our Lady belle   .   .   .   .   .   .   ij d.

Item, payde for mendynge of a wayle to the first mas belle   ij d.

Item, payde for vij. lynkes to visith withealle   .   iij s. vij d.

Item, for a quier of paper   .   .   .   .   iij d.

Item, to m^r Wyatt for keypinge our boke   .   .   viij d.

Item, payde for glasynge on the north syde the steple   .   iij s. iiij d.

Item, for straynyng the newe gable and settynge up   iiij d.

Item, for mendynge the for belle whele   .   .   iiij d.

    Summa totalis of reparacons   iij. li. xij s. v d. ob.

Item, payde to Troytes wife for a dossen of wax for the
    pascalle .   .   .   .   vij s.

Item, payde for makynge the pascalle   .   .   .   ij s. vj d.

Item, for oyle to the pascalle   .   .   .   .   ij d.

Item, for woode and faggottes to make the pascalle   .   iiij d.

Item, spent on them that made the pascalle   .   .   x d.

Item, payde for pynnes and nayles to the sepulcre   .   iij d.

Item, to Thomas Season for makynge a new claper and
    mendynge the olde claper .   .   .   .   .   vj d.

Item, more to hym for makynge the allelmas [1] upon the
    pascalle opon Easter day and paper to make them   ix d.

Item, paid for treselle and a corde to the organs   .   ij d.

Item, payde for a mase boke .   .   .   .   v s.

Item, payde for mendynge the chymes at ij. tymes, and
    wyer for the same, and the sprynge of them ano-
    ther tyme, and a bawdryck .   .   .   .   iij s. v d.

Item, payde to ser Richarde Cuper for makynge the ca-
    napie over the sacrament upon Corpus Christi day,
    and pyns and tackes to the same .   .   .   x d.

Item, payde to Thomas Season and John Tayler for shut-
    tynge [2] the belle ropes at dyvers tymes, and pycchinge
    them with pyche and talow .   .   .   iiij s. v d. ob.

Item, to Russhebery for mendynge the vestmentes, and
    for ij. stokes [3] and a hallf of locram to lyne them
    withalle .   .   .   .   .   .   iij s. vij d.

Item, to Richarde Kerver for mendynge the belle while [4]   iij d.

---

[1] The reading of this word is rather doubtful; perhaps it should be *alleluias*.

[2] The word *to shot* or *to shut*, is frequently applied to the bell ropes in the course of these accounts. It perhaps means to piece or mend them when broken. The word is sometimes used in the sense of to strengthen.   [3] yards?

[4] Wheel. This orthography is rather curious, as it would seem to show that the *i* was often pronounced as *e*. It is supposed that in Anglo-Saxon the vowels were pronounced as they are now in German and French, and in most of the continental languages, and that this continued to be the case in Old English down to a rather late date. The period of transition may have been as late as the beginning of the sixteenth century.

Item, to Thomas Season for mendynge the borde over the
    rode and nayles .   .   .   .   .   .   iiij d.

Item, for charcolles to sense withalle on hey dayes . iij d.

Item, payde to William Geyres for mendynge the stocke
    of the belle .   .   .   .   vj d.

Item, for mendynge the handylles of the belles at tymes viij d.

Item, payde for a locke and hynges to the church yearde
    dore .   .   .   .   vj d.

Item, payde to Thomas Season for mendynge the parishe
    bere .   .   .   .   viij d.

Item, payde to hym more for mendynge the ledes and
    sowder for the same .   .   .   .   ij s. iiij d.

Item, payde for ij. belle ropes .   .   .   xx d.

Item, to mr wardene for synginge bred this yere . iij s. iiij d.

Item, to mr Wyatt for takynge payne for us this yere viij d.
            Summa iij li. xvij s. j d. ob.

Receyttes of the parishe by Willyam Chelmycke and Lewys Crowther, churche wardens.

Receyvede at our entrye of John Clee and Howelle
    Glover, church wardens .   .   .   .   . ij s. viij d.

Receyvede at Easter for the pascalle .   .   .   . xxix s. vj d.

Receyvede of Watter Smycokes for the rest of mr Hares
    berialle .   .   .   . iij s. iiij d.

Receyvede of Thomas Heyton for his fathers berialle vj s. viij d.

Receyvede for the berialle of mr Rogers .   . vj s. viij d.

Receyvede of mrs Poton for the rest of her pewe . xx d.

Receyvede of John Lane ffor his wyfes grave . . vj s. viij d.

Receyvede of our gatherynge boke of the parishe, as
    aperythe .   .   .   . xiij s. x d.

Item, of the executors of Sybble late wife of John Lane,
    for her grave .   .   .   .   . vj s. viij d.

Item, sett to William Benson a pewe by the rode chanselle, by the consent of m^r bayliffes, receyvede of
hym for the same . . . . . . xx d.

Item, recevide of William Chelmyke for incresynge a pew
of Thomas Rascalle a fote of lenthe, and for that
charges the sayde Chelmyk most have the other half
of Thomas Rascalle pew by ther bothe consentes,
receyvede of hym for the gronde . . . iiij d.

Item, sett to Lewys Philipes and Lewys Crowther a pewe
wiche of late was Richarde Berys pewe, receyvede of
hym for the same . . . . . . iij s. iiij d.

Receyvede of master Sherman for that he was left at the
gret law day for plowenge a close in Gawforde [1] that
shulde have ben comyn that yere, whiche was geven
to the churche . . . . viij s.

Summa, iiij li. xj s. allocatur iij li. xvij s. j d. ob.
et sic debent super compotum, xiij s.

Memorandum, this day and at this accounte grauntyde by Lewys
Phillipes, one of the baylifes, and Lewys Crowther, one of the
late churche wardens and now on of the accountantes, on pewe
whiche late was Richarde Beries, for whiche sayde pewe the
sayde Philipes hath relasyde iij s. iiij d., parcelle of the debet
that the churche restede in his dett when he was churche warden,
and the sayd Crother payde for his parte iij s. iiij d., whiche is
payde, as apperithe by this accountt.
ffinis.

[1] See before, the note on p. 20. The land appears to have been given to the church
with a condition that it should not be ploughed the first year.

The charges susteignide by William Hoke and Thomas
Coxe, churche wardens of the parishe churche of
Ludlow, in anno secundo regni regis E. vj", as
folowithe, viz.

Anno Domini 1548.

In primis, to Thomas Taylor for his ffee for blowinge the
organs . . . . ij s. viij d.
Item, for xj. pounde of smalle candelles for the first masse,
wherof viij. li. after ij d. the pound, and iij. li. after
ij d. ob. the pounde . . . . . xxiij d. ob.
Item, to Thomas Season for shottynge [1] the belle rope ij.
tymes . . . . iiij d.
Item, to the sayde Thomas for shottynge the first belle
rope and for ix ringes for the highe aulter clothe
and the clothe that hangithe over the organs . v d.
Item, to the sayde Thomas for mendynge of ij. panes of
glasse, on in the vestry and thother in our Lady
chapelle . . . . xvj d.
Item, to the sayde Thomas for the while [2] of the first belle xvj d.
Item, to the sayde Thomas for shottinge the gret gable
rope . . . . iiij d.
Item, to the sayde Thomas and Newelles for pentinge [3]
of the roode lofte . . . . . xxvj s. viij d.
Item, to the sayde Thomas and others for takynge downe
of the roode and the images . . . . vj s. viij d.
Item, to Agnes Troyte, wido, for xvj li. of waxe to
make the pascalle after v d. every pounde . . vj s. viij d.

---

[1] I suppose, splicing the rope. [2] Wheel.

[3] If this means painting, it is rather curious that so much money should have been
spent on painting the rood-loft just at this period, when the church was on the eve of
being defaced by the removal of so much of its Romish furniture, as we see in the very
next entry.

Item, to the saide Agnes and William Powes, for the
makynge of the sayde pascalle after xv d. a pece   ij s. vj d.

Item, for oyle and for on sheme [1] of woode to the sayde
pascalle . . . .   iiij d.

Item, for brekfast after the makynge of the sayde pascalle   xij d.

Item, for di. a m. of singinge brede [2] . . . .   ij d. ob.

Item, for an edge to stay the Byble upon the deske .   ij d.

Item, to Stephen Knyght for mendynge the locke of the
church doore and for a key to the cofer in our
Lady chauncelle . . . .   v d.

Item, to Richarde Halle for his yeres wages . .   xx d.

Item, for nayles to hange up clothes when the images was
pullede downe . . . .   iiij d.

Item, to William Gittens for a new lader . . .   ij d.

Item, for ij. bandes of iron withe nayles to William Gittens, and the ij. boordes that where put upon the
pore mans chest, and for the workemanship therof to
hym . . . .   xiiij d.

Item, for a roppe to our Lady belle and a register to the
Bible . . . .   xv d.

Item, for a Bible for our partt . . . . . vij s. viij d.

Item, for v. lynckes to Agnes Troytt . . iij s. vj d.

Item, for di. a m. of singinge brede [2] . . .   ij d. ob.

Item, for xxx. pownde of sowder, and to the plymmar
and his man, and for v. days werke upon the leedes,
after vj d. the day, and the man v d. the day   xiiij s. vij d.

Ande for a quarter and vj li. of leede . . . . ij s. j d. ob.

Item, for ix. bushelles of colis [3] . . . .   ix d.

Item, to Richarde Swanson for mendynge the cover of
the ffont . . . .   v d.

---

[1] Load.

[2] *Singing-bread* was the name for the consecrated wafers, of which we here see that
half a thousand cost twopence halfpenny.

[3] Coals—no doubt, charcoal.

Item, to Season for shottinge the first belle rope . ij d.

Item, for iij. maylinge [1] coordes to hange up the vaile in
the quyre afore the alter . . . . . iij d.

Item, for nayles to mende the while [2] of the first belle . ij d.

Item, for vj. rynges [3] of lyme to pargitt the ledes . xij d.

Item, to Thomas Cocke and his man for a dayes worke
upon the syde leedes in pargettinge the same . xj d.

Item, to Steven Knyght for mendynge the locke of the
leedes dore . . . . :d.

Item, to Richarde Tomlyns for makynge our sertificatt
to the visitors [4] at ther beinge here . . xij d.

Item, to Thomas Hony for his flee . . . . xij d.

Item, for nayles and pynnes to make the sepulcre . iiij d.

Item, for a m. of synginge bredde . . . . v d.

Item, to the decons for rynginge day belle after Easter
at Mr baylifes commaundyment . . . . xij d.

Item, to Thomas Rushebury for mendinge the chymes
at ij. tymes. . . . . viij d.

Item, for ij. hanginge lockes for the pore man chest . xij d.

Item, to John Shrawley for pentynge [5] the clothe that
hangithe bifore the highe aulter and and a other in
our lady chapelle . . . . . . xx d.

Item, to Coke for whitlymynge the churche ij. dayes
worke, and for a busshelle and a whop [6] of lyme . xv d. ob.

Item, to William Marteyne for a dayes worke makynge
the rode loft playne [7] . . . . . . vj d.

Item, to the deacons for ther pounde of waxe at Ester iiij d.

---

[1] Perhaps, for binding.   [2] Wheel.

[3] Six rings of lime, to parget or rough-cast the leads. The word *ring*, as a measure of
quantity, appears to be entirely obsolete.

[4] The king's visitors, who were sent here to examine the amount of superstitious usages
existing in the church, and into the claims of the guild.

[5] Painting.

[6] This appears also to be another popular name for a measure the exact meaning of
which is now lost. *. . . , . . ~~~o , ... ?*

[7] i. e. defacing the superstitious figures which adorned it.

Item, for half a new roppe, and for shottynge the same,
and a roppe for the organs . . . . xiij d.

Item, to Steven Knyght for a whop of iron to the barrelle of the chymes . . . . . . ij d.

Item, for mendynge the tabernacles, and for sowinge
the aulbez at Ester, and for weshinge of the same xij d.

Item, for ij m. of synginge brede at Ester . . . x d.

Item, to Thomas Taylor for coverynge the grave over
the prisoners . . . . ij d.

Item, distributede to the poore at Whitsontyde . . ij s. iiij d.

Item, to Geres and Swift for takynge downe of m^r
Wyattes chancelle[1] . . . . . . xij d.

Item, for cariage of xv. lode of stones to William Hoke
to the Galforde . . . . ii s. viij d.

Item, to Richarde Tomlyns for makynge our loke . viij d.

Summa, v li. viij s. x d. ob.

Receytes of the sayde churche wardens the saide yere.

In primis, of John Belle and William Clonton late
churche wardens . . . . . . xj d.

Item, of Robert Mollyngre and David ap Richard for the
lofte that saynt George stode one . . . vj s.

Item, of Thomas Hony for the image of saynt George
that stode in the chapelle . . . . . xviij d.

Item, of John Coxe for a volt that the saide image stode
in . . . . iijs. iiij d.

---

[1] It would hardly be possible at present to identify the exact site of the different chan-
cels and chapels in our church mentioned in these entries. My friend Mr. R. Kyrke
Penson, who is better acquainted with the history of the fabric of Ludlow church than
anybody else I know, and whom I have consulted on this subject, informs me that " the
only point about which there appears to be any certainty is that the Lady Chapel was on
the south of the church. No one has been able to make out where St. George stood.
There were chapels at intervals, as is evident from the existing piscinas, down the north
and south aisles, and possibly St. George and St. Margaret may have stood in them.
Beawpy's chapel is a puzzle, because the two church aisles which might be called chapels
are known to be St. John's and the Lady Chapel."

Item, of William Philipes for a image of Jhesus that
stode in Beawpie [1] chapelle. . . . . x d.

Item, of the sayde William for a tabernacle that saynt
Margett stode in . . . . vj d.

Item, of John Season for ij. voltes that stode in our
lady chapelle . . . . xx d.

Item, of Walter Rosse for the dragon that the image of
saynt George stode upon . . . . . vij d.

Item, for the tabernacle of the image of saynt Kateryne
stode in of Gillmyn . . . . . . vj d.

Item, of Walter Taylor for the case that stode in Try-
nitie chancelle . . . . ij s. ij d.

Item, of Lewis Crother for the tabernacle that saynt
Anne stode in . . . . viij d.

Item, of Thomas Cother for the olde case of the organs xij d.

Item, for our parte of the olde Byble . . . iij s. iiij d.

Item, of Stephene Knyght, for a quarter and x li. of
iron . . . . iiij s. iiij d.

Item, of William Bradshaw for iiij. standardes weynge
a c and d. and xxvj li. . . . . . xxiiij s.

Item, at Easter . . . . xxxv s.

Item, of Stephen Knyght for a quarter and xiiij. li. of
olde iron . . . . iij s. vj d.

Item, rec. of Burge Jenyns, widow, for her husbandes
grave . . . . vj s. viij d.

Item, of Robert Mason for an other grave . . vj s. viij d.

Item, of Richard Handley for Leawis ap Bede grave . vj s. viij d.

Item, of William Hoke for a pew by the rode chauncelle . . . . ij s.

[1] Churchyard the poet. in his Worthines of Wales, says that Beawpy was buried near
the Font, and gives the following account of him :—

"Yet Beawpy must be nam'd, good reason why,
For he bestow'd great charge before he dyde
To kepe poore men, and now his bones doth lye
Full nere the font, upon the foremost side."

Item, of Thomas Coxe for half the pew withe Robert
    Adies   .   .   .   .   xij d.
            Summa   .   .   vj li. ij s. xj d.
        So that the accountauntes rest in dett to the churche
            upon this accounte   .   .   .   .   xiiij s. j d. ob.

                    ffinis.

Costes and charges done by us, William Benson and
    Richarde Stanwey, churche wardens of Ludlowe,
    anno regni regis Edwardi sexti Dei gratia, etc.,
    tercio. Anno Domini, 1549.

In primis, to Thomas Season for pavynge of saynt John
    chauncelle, for lyme, and for mendynge the chymes
    and the cloke   .   .   .   .   ij s. iiij d.
Item, payde to Richard Halle for swepynge the churche   vj d.
Item, to Thomas Taylor for blowinge the organs   .   viij d.
Item, to Rushbury for mendynge the chymes   .   .   ix d.
Item, payde for makynge clene the stear goynge up to
    the belles   .   .   .   .   iiij d.
Item, to John Taylor for mendynge of a belle rope   .   ij d.
Item, payde for mendynge of the parish bere   .   .   vj d.
Item, payde for mendynge of the grate   .   .   ij d.
Item, for ij. lode of lyme   .   .   .   .   .   .   ix d.
Item, for a bawdrike to the secounde tenor   .   .   xij d.
Item, for a new belrope to the same belle   .   .   .   xij d.
Item, payde for vij li. of waxe to make the pascalle   .   iiij s. viij d.
Item, payde for the parishe bookes, viz. iiij Mase bookes,
    one Paraffraces, and viij Salters   .   .   .   xxxvj s.
Item, for sowynge the albus and for threde   .   .   .   viij d.
Item, to Sir William Wyat for kepynge the parishe
    booke   .   .   .   .   xij d.

Item, to Thomas Season for mendynge of the belle rope
    and settynge up of them at dyvers tymes . . ijs. ijd.
Item, payde for a lynke and a tapur to the hie aulter . xij d.
Item, payde to the barbors for makynge of our pascalle ij s. vjd.
Item, for the brekfast at the makynge of the pascalle . xij d.
Item, for xiij li. of candelles .   .   .   . ij s. ix d. ob.
Item, for a li. of wier and a half and on j d. to mendthe
    chymes and the cloke at dyvers tymes . . . xiiij d. ob.
Item, for a belrope for the secounde belle . · . xxij d.
Item, payde for singinge brede .   .   .   .   . xiiij d.
Item, for makynge of the hynges to the church yate . iij d.
Item, payde for a huk .   .   .   .   .   . j d.
Item, for a lok to the same .   .   .   . ij d. ob.
Item, for a tapur to the first masse . · . vj d.
Item, payde for ij. lynkes .   .   .   .   . xij d.
Item, to Halle for nayles .   .   .   .   . j d.
Item, for ij. cordes to hange lyght at Christmas . . ij d.
Item, for pyns to pyn the aulter cloth at Christmas . j d.
Item, for a belrope for the first belle .   .   . xiiij d.
Item, payde for cordes to the organs .   .   . ij d.
Item, payde for ij. sheme [1] of lyme .   .   .   . ix d.
Item, payde for a lynk .   .   .   .   .   . vij d. ob.
Item, for whipcorde to hange the cloth before the hye
    aulter .   .   .   . ij d.
Item, payde for a ladder to go up to the clok . . iiij d.
Item, to Thomas Season for fachynge home the church
    ladder whiche was lent before we com in office . vj d.
Item, for paper to pryk songes in for the churche . ij d.
Item, to John Lyngran for settynge the cover over the
    pylpitt .   .   .   . xx d.
Item, for a forme for folkes to sytt upon .   . viij d.
Item, to Thomas Dik for whitlyme [2] the churche . ij d.
Item, for shiftynge of the organs into the hie aulter . ij d.

---

[1] Load. See before, p. 34.
[2] White-liming. or whitewashing, the church walls.

Item, to Thomas Season and Thomas Dyk for parget-
    tynge the leedes on bothe sides .   .   .   xx d.

Item, payde for oyle to the pascalle .   .   .   iij d.

Item, to Richarde Halle for makynge clene of the leedes
    and beynge [1] with them .   .   .   .   .   ij d.

Item, to the sayde Richarde for his quarteryege for
    swepynge of the church for iij. quarters .   .   xij d.

Item, for mendynge of the levis anont the college dore   vj d.

Item, for the makynge of our boke to gether our quar-
    terege .   .   .   .   iiij d.

Item, for mendynge of the pypes of the organs to John
    Broke and Thomas Season .   .   .   .   . ij s. viij d.

Item, paide for makynge a hand to our lady belrope .   iiij d.

Item, paide for mendynge the parishe bere   .   .   iiij d.

Item, to Richard Halle for blowynge the organs for iij.
    quarters .   .   .   .   ij s.

Item, for shottynge of the seconde tenor claper .   .   iiij d.

Item, for mendynge the chymez and the cloke to Tho-
    mas Season .   .   .   .   xx d.

Item, paide Thomas Season and his boy for iiij. days
    worke about the glasen wyndowis in the churche   iij s.

Item, payde for a lynk .   .   .   .   .   x d.

Item, paide for glase and leede .   .   .   .   ij s. vj d.

Item, for the keypynge of our boke alle the yere and the
    makynge of hym .   .   .   .   .   .   xij d.

            Summa allo[a]   .   .   iiij li. xj s.

Receites by us the saide church wardenes as here after folowith.

In primis, of Thomas Beadow wif for a pew rowme wher
    Bewpies chancelle was .   .   .   .   xviij d.

---

[1] It is not quite clear in the MS. whether the first letter of this word be b or l, but it seems to be the former.

Item, rec. of Laurance Becke for iiij. bordes   .   .   xij d.

Item, rec. of John Belle for xx. pyllars of m^r Wyat
chauncelle .   .   .   . iij s. iiij d.

Item, rec. of Rees ap Thomas for xvj. short bordes   .   xx d.

Item, rec. of John Rose for a kervide borde   .   .   vj d.

Item, rec. of Moris Phillipes for iiij. pyllars of m^r Wyat
chancelle and for a border   .   .   .   .   xij d.

Item, rec. of John Lokier for his wyf pytt   .   . vj s. viij d.

Item, rec. for Thomas Bowidon pitt   .   . vj s. viij d.

Item, rec. of the parishe ther quarterege   .   . . xij s. iiij d.

Item, rec. of the Easter boke   .   .   .   . xxxij s. vj d.

Item, rec. for ropes, bordes, and olde tymber   .   ij s. j d.

Item, rec. of m^r Shorman for the breke closse   .   .   iiij s.

Item, rec. for Wylliam Partrich wifes pitt   .   . vj s. viij d.

Item, rec. for Robert Hoode pitt   .   .   .   . vj s. viij d.

Item, rec. of John Newton for the grounde that his
pew standes on, wher Cookes chancelle was   .   xvj. d.

Item, rec. of hym for tymber to make the pew   .   ij s.

Item, rec. of m^r Shorman Myglemas rent for the breke
closse   .   .   .   .   iiij s.

Item, rec. of Roger Meysy for an olde coffer   .   .   viij d.

Item, rec. of Richard Stanwey for the revercion of Margery Hoodes pew   .   .   .   .   .   .   xx d.

Summa   .   .   iiij li. xvj s. iij d.
and so the accountantes restith in dett to the
churche upon this accounte   .   v s. iij d.
Dett to the churche as her after folowith.

Item, rest in m^r Richarde Bradforde handes and William Partrighe of the last acount receites   .   .   xiiij s.

Item, for tymber that m^r Partriche hade not accountede
as yet   .   .   .   .   xvj d.

Item, of m^r Alsop for the pyllars of the rode chauncelle   xvj d.

Item, rest in Johan Troyte handes of the churche goodes
ij. dosson of waxe.

Item, more m^r Parteridge the yonger for the carvyde
  beame in the churche[1]   .   .   .   .   .
Item, more in thandes of William Benson for leedes that
  was in the hally water stoke weynge   .   .   .
                ffinis.

The boke of acounts of Antony Atkynson and Edward
  Cuper, church wardens, in the tyme of Richard.
  Langfford and Thomas Heyton, bayliffes of the
  towne of Ludlow, in the forthe yere of the rayne of
  our moste dread soveraigne lord Edwarde the sixt.
            Anno Domini 1550.

In primis, payd to John Lyngham for the makynge of
  a seat before the pilpitt in the church   .   .   .   v s.
Item, payd for xj. li. of candles, and on penieworth to
  serve to light in the churche and first comunion   .   xxiij d.
Item, for mendynge of Roger Meysy chamber wyndow   iiij d.
Item, for ij. belropes, the one to the first belle and the
  other to the secound belle   .   .   .   .   .   v s. ij d.
Item, to Thomas Season, for shotynge of thre belropes   vj d.
Item, payd for mendynge of the cloke and chymes, and
  for wier to the same   .   .   .   .   .   .   xij d.
Item, for ij. borden of roddes to the house[2] in the churche
  yeard   .   .   .   .   iiij d.
Item, for wyndynge[3] of the walles of the sayd howse   .   iij d.

[1] This was no doubt the beam the expenses of carving which are accounted for on a
former occasion. See p. 11.

[2] No doubt the old timber house still standing there, nearly facing the eastern end of
the church. The two burthens of rods were probably the laths or boards used in the
walls. This is the date to which we may perhaps trace the present building.

[3] It seems to mean plaistering, or something of that kind; see a few lines further on,
where it occurs again.

Item, for a lock to the yate in the churche yearde . iiij d.

Item, to Johan Troyt, for ij. tapers weyinge iij. pound
for the first mas . . . . ij. s.

Item, for lathes and nailes to mend the wyndowis in the
steple and other wher . . . . . ij d. ob.

Item, for mendynge of the loke of the churche dore at
ij. tymes . . . . iiij d.

Item, to Thomas Season, for gowinge up into the stiple
ij. wyndy nyghtes to save[1] the glase yn the wyndowis . . . . x d.

Item, payd to Thomas Season and Thomas Dyke for
makinge clene of the church walles within the
churche, and for whitlymynge the same . . iiij s.

Item, for makynge of the clapper to the fore belle ij.
tymes . . . . xxij d.

Item, payd for pytt lyme to the churche . . . vj d.

Item, to Thomas Season and Thomas Dyke, for pargettynge on the leedes for a day and an half . . ix d.

Item, to Thomas Season, for keypinge the cloke and
chymes, belwhiles,[2] belropes, and baudrikes,[3] by
the yere . . . . vj s. viij d.

Item, to William Powis, for the first masse belrope . vij d.

Item, to Thomas Season for a day and an half in sou-
deringe the leedes . . . . . . x d.

Item, payd for a li. and an half of sowdre . . . ix d.

Item, to Richard Halle for blowynge the organs and
swepynge the churche . . . . . iiij s. viij d.

Item, payd to Richard Tomlyns, for the parishe boke
wryttynge . . . . viij d.

Item, to Thomas Season, for mendynge of the glasen
wyndowis in the steple, and for a new pane . xx d.

---

[1] i. e. to protect.

[2] Bell-wheels.

[3] See this word explained in the note on p. 4.

Item, to the said Thomas for mendynge of saynt Kathe-
rine wyndow and for glase . . . . . vj s. viij d.
Item, for mendynge of saynt Margettes wyndow [1] . xx d.
Item, to the sayd Thomas, for ix. fote of new glasse to
the west wyndow in the stiple . . . vj s.
Item, to Thomas Season, for iiij. dais worke and an half
on the leedes . . . . ij s. iiij d.
Item, to hym for half a day at the whirle yate [2] anont
the college dore . . . . . . iiij d.
Item, for vij. li. of sowder bestowed upon the leedes iiij s. j d.
Item, payd for colles . . . . ij d.
Item, payd to William Gillis for carrege of ij. lodes of
cley to the house in the churche yeard . . viij d.
Item, to John James for wyndynge and dawbynge ther viij d.
Item, payd for iiij. borden of roodes . . . . viij d.
Item, to Richard Crosse for xix li. of yren to mend the
yelde belle clapper . . . . . ij s. iiij d. ob.
Item, to the sayd Richard for mendynge of the said
clapper . . . . ij s. viij d.
Item, for a hynge and the settynge on the yate in the
churche yard . . . . ij d.
Item, for lether to make a new bawdrike to the fore belle viij d.
Item, for vij li. of iron to the clapper of the for belle x d. ob.
          Summa . iij li. xij s. j d. ob.
Summa totalis of the receites, as apperithe, iiij li. ij s. vj d.
So the accountauntes owe the churche of this accounte x s. iiij d. ob.
Wherof they ar allowid for consideracions . . x d.
More dd. to the new churche wardens in money of John
Alsope, for that he owid to the churche for olde
tymber . . . . xvj d.

---

[1] I am not aware that there are any remains of this window at present. The figure of St. Margaret was probably represented in the stained glass.

[2] I presume a *whirle-gate* was what we call a turnstile. It probably led into the church-yard opposite (*onont*) the buildings of the College.

Item, received of Johan Troyte, ij. dossen and iiij. li.
of waxe

Item, of William Parteriche the yonger, for a karvid
beame . . . . ij s.

Item, of William Benson for d. c. lakkynge iiij. li. of leade.[1]

The receites by us the forsayd churche wardens, as here after ffolowith.

In primis, received of the Easter boke . . . xxx s.

Item, received for the images, of Richard Lloyde . xiij s. iiij d.

Item, received of William Parterige for a beame . xvj d.

Item, received of Richard Stanwey and William Benson, the rest of ther account the last yere . v s.

Item, received of m͏ʳ Wylliam Ffoxe for a barre of iron
weynge xxx li. . . . . . . iij s.

Item, received of m͏ʳ warden Langford, for his wif
grave . . . . vj s. viij d.

Item, received ffor the olde bookes in the churche of the
old service . . . . ij s. viij d.

Item, for tymber solde to m͏ʳ Passie and Leawys Philipes to make the new pewis . . . . xvj d.

Summa . . iij l. iij s. iiij d.

ffinis.

Costes and charges don by us, Robert Mason and Robert
Mollynger, churche wardens of Ludlow, in tempore
Thomas Blashfild and John Coxe tunc ballivis.
Anno Edwardi sexti quinto. Anno Domini 1551.

In primis, payd to John Lyngam, for iiij. days worke
after viij d. a day, for movinge the pilpett and
makynge seetes by the Trynitye chancelle . . ij s. iiij d.

Item, payd to his ij. men for iiij. dayes workyn ther . iiij s.

---

[1] For half a hundred lacking four pounds.

Item, payd to Thomas Bold and Thomas Dike, for vj.
    dais worke downe the aulters, after vij d. the day   vij s.

Item, payd for caryinge of ramelle [1] out of the churche
    to iiij. laborars, after vj d. the day, for xviij. dais   ix s.

Item, for leed to sowdre the pylpett   .   .   .   .   ij d.

Item, for bordes to John Lyngam, for the Trinitie
    chancelle   .   .   .   .   xx d.

Item, to Thomas Beadow, for v. bordes to serve the table
    for the comynyan and the Trynytie chancelle, after
    ix d. the bord   .   .   .   .   .   .   iij s. ix d.

Item, paid for nayles.   .   .   .   .   .   ij d.

Item, paid for sawynge the frame to the said table   .   x d.

Item, paid to a workman for coverynge of Richard Wes-
    ton wif grave, and for mendynge of the hooles in
    saynt John chancelle.

Item, paid to John Taylor for mendynge of ij. belropes   vj d.

Item, to ij. women for makynge clene of the churche   iiij d.

Item, paid to William Gers and Roger Swyft, for mak-
    ynge of the pewis by the rode chauncelle, for vj.
    dais after vij d. the day   .   .   .   .   vij s.

Item, to Thomas Dike, for mendynge of an hoole ther
    as our Lady aulter dyd stand   .   .   .   iij d.

Item, to Richard Kerver, for makynge the comynyon
    table, and for nayles   .   .   .   .   .   iiij s. vij d.

Item, to John Blont for mendynge of a seet in the Tri-
    nytie chauncelle   .   .   .   .   .   .   iiij d.

Item, paid to ij. plommers, for iiij. dais and a di. worke
    on our Lady chauncelle and saynt Margrettes chaun-
    celle, after viij d. the day   .   .   .   .   iiij s. viij d.

Item, to the sayd plommers for sowdering   .   .   .   ix s.

Item, to John Broke for mendynge ij. peyre of organs   .   xij d.

Item, for a hynge and a hoke to the churche dore   .   iiij d.

[1] Rubbish.

Item, paid to the dekyns [1] for rynginge of day belle . xij d.

Item, to Richard Halle for his yeres wages for the blowynge the organs and for swepynge the churche v s. iiij d.

Item, for ij. shem of wood to the plommers . . vj d.

Item, for pesynge of the for belle clapper to Richard
Crosse . . . . xij d.

Item, for the dressynge of the bellmons belle xx d.

Item, paid for rushes [2] to the Trinitie chancelle . . ij d.

Item, for makynge of the ij. beeris and for nailes . . iiij s. iiij d.

Item, to Thomas Dike and Thomas Bold, for leynge
of the aulter stonys in the midle of the churche . vj s. ij d.

Item, paid for a rope to the secound tenor . . . iiij s. viij d.

Item, paid for a rope to our Lady belle . . . ij s. iiij d.

Item, for iiij. ropes to the organs . . . . viij d.

Item, to Thomas Season for his yeres wages for the
chymes and the cloke . . . . . viij s.

Item, to Stephyn Knyght, for mendynge the churche
dore loke . . . . ij d.

Item, paid for viij. li. of candles . . . . ij s.

Item, to Thomas Season for mendynge the secound
tenour while . . . . ij s.

Item, for ij. days worke about the churche house, and
for rodes . . . . xij d.

Item, paid the decons for readynge the first chapter . iij s. iiij d.

Summa . v li. ix d.

Receites by us, Robert Mason and Robert Mollynger,
churche wardens, as here after fowloeth,

In primis, of William Philipes toward the movinge of
the pilpett . . . . vj s. viij d.

Item, received of mr John Alsop for an old dett dew to
the churche . . . . xvj d.

_____

[1] Deacons.   [2] To cover the floor.

Item, received of Richard Lloyd for a pew place next
to John Newton . . . . . .   ij s.

Item, received of William Phillipes for a pew place .   xx d.

Item, received of Anthoni Atkynson for a pew place
where the pilpett stod . . . . .   iij s. iiij d.

Item, received of Robert Bradoke for a pew place behynde the Trinitie chauncelle . . . .   iij s. iiij d.

Item, received of Richard Kever for a pew place be-
side the said chauncelle . . . . .   ij s.

Item, received of William Bradshaw and Richard Stau-
wey for the agmentynge of ther pew . . .   ij s.

Item, of Richard Rogers for thend of a pew with his
brother-in-law . . . . . .   xx d.

Item, received of John Clee and John Belle for a pew
late Jane Fernes . . . . . .   xiij s. iiij d.

Item, received of William Huke for a pew place next to
Howelle ap Rees . . . . . .   ij s.

Item, received of Richard Adams for a pew place next
to mʳ Cothers . . . . . .   ij s.

Item, received of Thomas Beadw and Robert Mason
for a pew place in the rode chauncelle . . .   vj s. viij d.

Item, received of William Benson for the agmentynge
of his pew ther . . . . . .   ij s.

Item, received of John Cox for a pew, late my lady
Croftes . . . .   xij d.

Item, received of Robert Mollynger for a pew place next
to John Gwynes . . . . . .   xij d.

Item, received for another pew place next behynde mʳ
Bark, wiche Robert Mason hathe . . .   xij d.

Item, received for old brasse of the churche, conteynyng
xlv li. . . . .   xv s.

Item, received of John Belle for ij. peces of old tymber   iij s. iiij d.

Item, received of Robert Mollynger for ij. peces of old
tymber . . . .   iij s. iiij d.

Item, of the said Robert for a old coffer at the Trenytie
    chauncelle . . . .   ij s.
Item, received of m^r doctour Leyson for the burialle of
    his man . . . . vj s. viij d
Item, received of Richard Weston for his wif pitt . vj s. viij d.
Item, received of my lady Townisend for the burialle
    of her doughter . · . . . . . vj s. viij d.
Item, received of Alis Rogers for stones out of the
    churchyard . . . . xvj d.
Item, received for the quarterege boke, as it dothe appere
    by a boke . . . . xxxix s. iiij d.
Item, received of Edward Cowper for a pew that was
    mistres Whittulle . . . . . . ij s.
Item, received of the old church wardens of the last
    account . . . . ix s. vj d.
    Summa of the receyttes of this yere, as apperith true by
        this boke . . . vij li. viij s. x d.
Wherof they ar allowyd for my lady Towneshendes
    doughters grave . . . . vj s. viij d., and for
    the church wardens pew place ij s.   . . viij s. viij d.
So remayneth clere to the churche upon this accounte   vij li. ij d.
Wherof allowyd to the accountauntes for reparacions of
    the churche, and other necessarye charges, as appe-
    rithe by bylle . . . . v li. ix d.
        So restithe clere . . xxxix s. vj d.
    Whiche is paid to the churche wardens of new electid.
Item, more to receive of ʾJohan Troyte for ij. dossen of
    waxe
Item, more to receive of William Parteriche the yonger
    for a karvyd beame . . . . . . ij s.
Item, more to receive of William Benson for di. c.
    lakkinge iiij. li. of leade.
              finis.

The boke of account of John Hullond and Thomas
Franke, churche wardens of the parishe churche of
Ludlow, anno Edwardi sexti sexto.
Anno Domini 1552.

In primis, to Watter Rosse, for his pew . . . ij s. vj d.
Item, to Thomas Season, for mendynge the secounde belle
whele and for makynge of a hand . . . viij d.
Item, payd for nayles to the table and to the whele . vij d.
Item, payd to the plommer for mendynge the leedes of
the churche . . . . xij s. vj d.
Item, paid to the glasiar for glasynge the wyndos xxviij s. vj d.
Item, paid for xxxij. li. of leed to serve the glasier . iiij s.
Item, for iiij. li. of sowder, to William Bradshaw . ij s.
Item, paid for iij. li. and a half of sowder to the glasier ijs. iiij d.
Item, paid for ij. sheme and a half of wood to Richard Parkes x d.
Item, paid for iij. sheme of wood . . . . xij d.
Item, for ij. cordes to bend the glasiars ladders . . ij d.
Item, paid for rossen and salt . . . . ij d.
Item, paid for iij. belropes . . . . . iiij s. xj d.
Item, for makynge of Hew Davis pew, and for a borde xij d.
Item, for cadis and nayles to the communion table . j d.
Item, paid for settynge up of the stear goynge up to the
cloke . . . . xij d.
Item, for mendynge the for belle whele . . . ij d.
Item, paid for wier to the chymes . . . . v d.
Item, for whitlymynge the churche, to Lewis the
tylour . . . . x d.
Item, paid for lyme . . . . . . ix d.
Item, paid for makynge of the churche yate, and for
tymber and nayles, to William Gyttyns . . xiiij d.
Item, for makynge the walle at the churche house, and
for rodes . . . . iiij d

Item, paid to Thomas Rushbery for settynge the chymes   vij s.

Item, to the sayd Thomas for rynginge day belle .   .   xij d.

Item, paid to Richard Halle for his wages .   . vj s. viij d.

Item, paid for candles to serve the churche   .   iij s.

Item, paid for mendynge the bere at ij. tymes   .   .   v d.

Item, paid for swepynge seynt John chauncelle ij. tymes   iij d.

Item, for settynge a barre to the churchgrate and a bost[1] for hym . . . .   iij d.

Item, for mendynge the texe in the hye chauncelle   .   ob.

Item, to Lewis Gwyn for ij. days worke in the churche   xviij. d.

Item, to John Smyth for ij. sheme of wod to the plommer . . . .   ij d.

Item, for candles and nayles to the plommer   .   .   ij d.

Item, paid to the plommer for vij. li. and di. of sowder   v s.

Item, paid to the plommer and his man for a day and di.   xx d.

Item, payd to Rushberie . . . . iij s. iiij d.

Item, payd for ij. bookes to the churche   .   .   . vj s. viij d.

Item, payd for brede and wyne .   .   .   .   xiiij d.

Item, payd for xvj. li. of leed to ley on the churche   .   ij s.

         Summa   .   vj li. vij s. viij d.

Receites by us the said churche wardens, as here after ffolowithe.

In primis, received by thandes of m^r Blashfild and m^r Cokes . . . . xxxix s. vj d.

Item, received of Edward Cuper   .   .   .   xvj d.

Item, received of Lewis Capper .   .   .   . xiij s. iiij d.

Item, received of Richard Ffern for a pew ground   .   ij s.

Item, received of John ap Ywen for a pew ground   .   xx d.

Item, received of Robert Draper for a clothe   .   . ij s. iiij d.

Item, sold Thomas Rushbiry, a clothe for   .   .   vj s.

Item, received for the pitt of John Smyth clerke   vj s. viij d.

Item, received for the pitt of John Clee   .   . vj s. viij d.

[1] This is a word with which I am unacquainted, but perhaps it is a corruption of *boss*.

Item, received of John Sutton and William Carpynter
for a pew place . . . .   ij s.
Item, received of Edmond Bolland for a pew place .   ij s.
Item, for a pew place beneth Robert Mollyngers pew,
for John Holland and Thomas Ffranke   .   .
Item, received of William Benson for a pew place .   xij d.
Item, received of the parishners for ther quarterage   xxxij s. viij d.
   Summa of the receytes . . v li. xvij s. ij d.
    And so they accountauntes restethe in dett to
    the churche upon this account   .   .   ix s. ij d.
    More in the handes of Johan Troyte wydow,
    one dossen and xj li. of waxe, prece.
    Wherof allowyd to Thomas Rushburie for
    dyvers consideracions .   .   .   .   iij s. vj d.
    So restithe   .   .   .   vj s.
    More to be received of Edmond Shermond
    for the bryk closse due at Michelmas last   viij s.
     ffinis.

Costes and charges don by us, Watter Symcokes and
  William Beadow, church wardens, anno primo
  Marie regine.
     Anno Domini 1553.

In primis, to John Thacher, for weshynge of the walles
and for mendynge of the walles .   .   .   .   viij d.
Item, to William Gyttyns for makynge of the knelinge
place about the Lordes table, for nayles and blockes   vj d.
Item, for the makynge of v. bawdrekes to the belles, and
stuf to ytt .   .   .   .   x s. ij d.
Item, payd to Richard Halle   .   .   .   .   .   vj s. viij d.
Item, ffor candles to the prestes, to the decon, and to
James Wiltes   .   .   .   .   .   ij s. vj d.

Item, paid for movinge of the pewis, for nailes and work-
manshipe, and for other stuff, the xviij. day of
Februari . . . . ix s. x d.
Item, paid for wier to the chymes and the cloke . xij d.
Item, paid for makynge of the arme of the bere, and for
mendynge of the bere at ij. tymes, and the leof of
the grate at tymes . . . . . . xj d.
Item, for a locke to the churche yate . . . . iiij d.
Item, paid for the makynge of Thomas Rushburi
sirples¹ at ij. tymes . . . . . . ix d.
Item, paid for wyne and bred on Palme Sonday evyn,
and on the day . . . . xxj d.
Item, for xxxj. quartes of wyne from Palme Sonday un-
tille the Easter wike,² and for bred . . . viij s.
Item, to Rushbury for ryngynge of day belle . . xij d.
Item, paid to Richard Kerver, for iiij. bellcropes and
di. and for the crosse staffe . . . . viij s.
Item, paid for mendynge the aulter clothe . . . ij d.
Item, paid for iiij. cordes to the organs at dyvers tymes iiij d.
Item, for makynge of the fformes in saynt Margettes
chansellc, for the leadz ther . . . . xvj d.
Item, paid for nayles to the same . . . . vj d.
Item, paid for fformes to the same . . . x d.
Item, to Rushbiry for mendynge of the chymes . ij s. ij d.
Item, to Stephen Knyght for his workmanship . . xvj d.
Item, for settynge a loke on the cloke house dore, and
for the loke . . . . iiij d.
Item, paid to John Barker for mendynge of the leedes
in the northe ile . . . . . . viij d.
Item, to Thomas Season for glasynge of the wyndowis
and for mendynge of the same . . . xxiij s. iiij d.
Item, payd for lyme . . . . xv d.
    Summa   iiij. li. v s. j d.

¹ Surplice.   ² week.

The receites of us the said churche wardens, as here after ffolowithe.

In primis, of m^r bayliffs, for the dettes of the last account . . . .   vj s.

Item, received of William Benson for Allhollon chaunselle . . . .   x s.

Item, received of John Belle for seynt Stevens chaunselle . . . .   vj s.

Item, of m^r bailiffes for ther pew . . . .

Item, of the chamberlene Edward Cupper for his pew .

Item, of Watter Symcokes and William Beadoo for ther pew . . . .

Item, received of Laurence Becke and Richard Parkes for ther pew place . . . . . .   iij s. iiij d.

Item, received of Humfry Hynton and John Sothern for ther pew place . . . . . .   xx d.

Item, received of John Gr. showmaker and John Gregory, for their pew place . . . . .   xx d.

Item, received of John Newton for an old tabernacle   xx d.

Item, received of Richard Carpynter for his pew ground   ij s.

Item, received of John Beado and John Brasyer for their pew ground . . . . . .   xx d.

Item, received of John Bubbe and Richard Adams for their pew place . . . .   ij s.

Item, received of Edward Dowghtie and Adam Maneley for their pew place . . . . . .   ij s.

Item, received of Richard Farre and William Tandy for ther pew place, iiij s. rec. . . . .   iiij s.

Item, received of John Gr. senior and Richard Gilmyn for ther pew place . . . . . .   xx d.

Item, received of William Eaton and [1] pew place . . . . . .   xx d.

[1] The blank is left in the original.

Item, received of Robert Covelle and John Wilson for
their pew place . . . . xviij d.
Item, received of Richard Cupper for his pew place . xij d.
Item, received of John Clee and Hew Cubley for ther
pew place . . . . xx d.
Item, received of m^r Shermond for the bryk close for
one year ended at Mychelmas last . . . viij s.
Item, received wyklie for the money called the charitie
money, after viij d. the wek for xxxij. wekes . xxj s. iiij d.
     Summa of alle the receytes of the churche
     wardens this yere . v li. ij s. j d.
Wherof they ar allowyd, as apperithe by bill iiij li. v s. j d.
So they rest indettid to the churche upon this
     account . . . . . xvij s.
More in thandes of Johan Troyte widow
one dossen x li. of waxe . . .
Of whiche said some of xvij s. ther is payd to
Richard Crose for mendynge the clapper of
the grett belle . . . . . . v s.
More to Thomas Season in parte of xxvj s. viij d. due to
hym for iiij. copes bought of hym and restored to
the churche, withe v s. of old dett, and for ij. latteyn
candelstickes . . . . xij s.
So ther restithe due to Thomas Season . . xiiij s. viij d.
           Finis.

Thomas Beadow and Thomas Blakbage, churche wardens
in the yere of John Taylor and Edmond Shermon,
bayliffes, anno primo et secundo Philipi et Marie.
Anno Domini 1554.

In primis, payd to Thomas Season, whiche the parishe
was indetted at our comynge to our office . . xv s. iiij d.
Item, to Richard Halle for his yeres wages . . . vj s. viij d.
Item to Thomas Season, for hanginge of the lampe
and for cordes . . . . . . xij d.

Item, to the sayd Thomas, for half a rope and for men-
dynge of the ropes . . . . . .   xij d.
Item, paid for candles at dyvers tymes . . .   xxij d.
Item, paid for mendynge of the grate . .   iiij d.
Item, paid for a tonaculle [1] to cary hally water . .   ij s. x d.
Item, for hangynge of the sauntes belle, and for the corde   ij d.
Item, paid for albis, cordes, and candles at Christemas .   xij d. ob.
Item, paid for makynge the hie aulter . . .   xj s.
Item, for mendynge of the ropes at master Langford
berynge . . . .   viij d.
Item, paid for mendynge of the ropes, and for pentynge [2]
over the hie aulter, and for makynge the ffoote to
the treselle . . . .   viij d.
Item, paid to William Powis for a rope and a lynke .   ij s. x d.
Item, for makynge clene of the grate, and for a tapur to
the first mase . . . .   xiij d.
Item, paid for a rope to the gild belle . . .   xx d.
Item, for a canape for the pyxe, and for a cord to the
organs . . . .   xvj d.
Item, paid for a belle rope . . . . .   xvj d.
Item, paid for the settynge up of the rood . . .   iiij d.
Item, paid for weshynge of the clothis . . .   iiij d.
Item, paid to iij. workmen for swepynge the churches walles ij s. ij d.
Item, paid for wyer to mend the chymes . . .   iiij d.
Item, paid for ffrankensence . .   ij d.
Item, paid for coolis [3] . .   iij d.
Item, paid for a tapur . . . . .   iij d.
Item, paid for tymber to the pascalle . . .   vj d.
Item, paid for a rope . . .   xviij d.
Item, paid for ij. bawdrikes . . . . .   xvj d.

---

[1] I have not met with this word in any sense which could be accepted here.   *Tonnycle*
is given in the Promptorium Parvulorum as the English name for one of the ecclesiastical vestments. Perhaps it is here merely the diminutive of *tonne*, or *tunne*, explained in
the Promptorium by the Latin *dolium*.

[2] The word here appears evidently to mean making a pentice.   [3] Coals.

Item, paid for a lynke to William Powis . . x d.

Item, for faggottes . . . . . . j d.

Item, for makynge the iee of the clapper . . . xiiij d.

Item, to Richard Swansey for iij. ropes . . . iiij s.

Item, paid for mendynge of the flonte . . iiij d.

Item, for a corde to the organs, and nayles . . ij d.

Item, for sawynge the tymber that went to the while

    of the belle . . . . ij d.

Item, paid to ij. workemen . . . . . vj d.

Item, paid for a lynke . . . . . viij d.

Item, paid for nayles . . . . . . ij d.

Item, for half a c. of cloute nayles . . . . iij d. ob.

Item, for a c. and an half of gret tackes . . . iij d.

Item, for nayles at on other tyme . . . . iij d. ob.

Item, paid for spyke nayles . . . . . j d.

Item, for a spoke of a while, to Thomas Season . ij d.

Item, paid for rydinge of the steres of the stiple . . ij d.

Item, paid to John Blunt for iiij. days worke . . iij s.

Item, paid for the reparacions of the belles, and for a new

    while, and for hangynge of the secound belle at the

    same tyme, to Thomas Season for v. days worke . iij s. iiij d.

Item, for the shutynge of the gild belle rope . . iiij d.

Item, for the hongynge of the pixe over the aulter . xiij d.

Item, paid for the cochynge of the belle, and for iron

    that went to the while . . . . . xiiij d.

Item, paid for ij. ropes to the organs . . . . ij d.

Item, for mendynge of the bere . . . . ij d.

Item, paid for bordes to the belle while . . . xij d.

Item, to a workeman for a days worke at the churche

    gate, and for mendynge of the pewis . . . viij d.

Item, paid for bordz and postes, with a lach to the gate xij d.

Item, for a rope to the organs . . . . j d.

Item, to mr Shermon for iiij. sheme of lyme . . xij d.

Item, paid the deken at Easter	xviij d.
Item, for porrelz[1] for albis	vj d.
Item, for shotynge of ij. ropez at Ester . . .	iiij d.
Item, for naylz and pynnez to the sepulcre . . .	v d.
Item, for pentynge of the post to the pascalle . .	vj d.
Item, paid to John Allen for gildynge of the rode .	xij s.
Item, for the settynge up of the rode and pullynge yt downe agaynne	xij d.
Item, paid to m[r] Blashfild for waxe	v s. vj d.
Item, paid for makynge of the pascalle . . .	xx d.
Item, to Richard Swansay for a pece of tymber to the pascalle, and for iiij. staffes to the canopie, and for the indeces, and for mendynge the bere . .	v s. viij d.
Item, for the crose clothe	iiij. d.
Item, for shottynge of iij. ropes, and settynge up ij. new ropes	vij d.
Item, for shottynge of iij. ropes, when the ronge bishop Samson in[2]	vj d.
Item, for mendynge of iij. ropes, when we dyd rynge at the mariage of the kynge[3]	vj d.
Item, paid for vj. flote of new glase in seynt Mergrettes chauncelle	iiij s.
Item, for mendynge more there	vj d.
Item, for mendynge of the glassen windowes in our Lady chauncelle and in Katerin chauncelle .	ij s.

---

[1] The exact spelling of this word is a little doubtful in the manuscript. . ˙. (ˈ. ¬

[2] This must be Richard Sampson Bishop of Lichfield, who had held the high office of Lord President of Wales and the Marches from 1543 to 1548, when on the accession of Edward VI. he was removed, but he was perhaps temporarily restored on the accession of Mary.

[3] Another hand has written over the line " *Ph*," *i. e.* Philippus. The marriage of Queen Mary with Philip of Spain took place on the 25th of July, 1554, with which day, which was now called the first day " of the first and second year of the reign of Philip and Mary," began the new regnal year, which will be found at the head of the present churchwardens' year.

Item, payd for shottynge of ij. ropes on Alhallen daye   iiij d.
Item, payd for makynge clenne of the church yerd   iiij d.
Item, payd for ij. poundes of candles .   .   .   v d.

       Summa   .   .   xlix s. vij d.
     Summa totalis   .   .   vj li. iiij s. x d. ob.

Receittes by us the forsaid churche wardens, to the use
   of the churche, as here after folowith.

In primis, receved of our quarterege boke, as hit dothe
   appere by our boke .   .   ,   .   .   . xxvj s. ij d.
Item, receved at Easter .   .   .   .   . xxxv s. vij d.
Item, receved of m^r Richard Langford for his fathers
   pytt .   .   .   . vj s. viij d.
Item, receved of the sayd m^r Langford for ij. pewis,
   whiche were his fathers .   .   .   .   . vj s. viij d.
Item, receved of m^r Debton for his dowghter pitt   vj s. viij d.
Item, receved of m^r Foxe and m^r Passy for a pew   iij s. iiij d.
Item, receved of m^r Barnabie and m^r Ellis for a pew   xiij s. iiij d.
Item, receved of m^r Shorman for a pew place at Al-
   hallon chauncelle .   .   .   .   .   . xij d.
Item, receved of Humfry Season for a pew place   .   xviij d.
Item, receved of Smalez pitt, servant to m^r justes   . vj s. viij d.

          Pittes unpaid.
Item, for Edward Cupper pitt .   .   .   .   . vj s. viij d.
Item, for Edward Colly pitt .   .   .   .   . vj s. viij d.
       Summa   .   .   vj li. xj d.
Summa of alle the receittes of the church wardens this
   yere .   .   .   . vj li. xj d.
Wherof they are allowid, as apperith by bille . v li. xix s. x d. ob.
         finis.

The boke of accomptes and charges layd out by us, Richard Farre and Laurence Becke, churche wardens elect and chossen for the yere of our Lord God 1555, by particulars as followythe.

In primis, delyvered the xxviij. day of November for the furst masse and to burne in the lamps ij li. of candelles . . . .   v d.

ij. ounces franke and sens[1] at . . . . .   j d.

To Rushebery to rynge courfur[2] ij li. candelles . .   v d.

Mor to the pristes, the xth day of December, for furst mase on pound candelles . . . . .   ij d. ob.

Paid for a sklyce[3] to cary fyer to the churche . .   x d.

Paid ffor mendynge of the locke and a new kaye for the stiple dore at . . . . . .   iij d.

Paid William Marten for iij. dayes worke removynge the pewis in the lower end of the churche, at x d.   ij s. vj d.

Paid Roger Swyfte for iij. dayes worke apon the same penys . . . .   ij s. iij d.

Paid Holand the carpender, for iij. dayes worke apon the same penys . . . .   ij s. iij d.

Paid for ij. bordes for the same penys, at 6d. . .   xij d.

For c. borde nayles for the same pewis . . .   x d.

Paid for iij. peyre hynges for the same at 4d. . .   xij d.

The xxiiij day of December for the fyrst mase j li. of candles . . . .   ij d. ob.

To Rusheberie, to burne in the vestrie on Christmas day in the mornynge, a bushelle of charcolles at .   iiij d.

And to hym, the same day, for the lampe j li. of candles . . . .   ij d. ob.

On new yeres even, ij. ounces ffranke and sens, at   j d.

---

[1] *i. e.* frankincense.   [2] curfew.

[3] In the dialects of the West of England a fireshovel is still called a *slice.*

The iiijth day of Januarii, to the pristes for the furst
    masse ij. pound candelles at 2d. ob. . . .   v d.
Paid for clensynge the leedes at . . . . .   iiij d.
A nelle and half dowles [1] to make iij. amysses at 14d.   xxj d.
For makynge and strynges for the same, at .   ij d.
A pound candelles for first mase . . . .   ij d. ob.
Paid for removinge the clocke to the secound tenor, and
    mendynge the whelle of the clocke . . .   ij s.
Paid Thomas Season, for shuttynge iij. of the belle ropes   vj d.
And to hym for mendynge the sencer . . .   iiij d.
Paid more to hym for shuttynge ij". belle ropes . .   iij d.
Paid Rushberi for mendynge ij°. coopis, on of red velvet,
    the other red sylke, and for apparalynge of ij°. albes   v d.
Paid Thomas Season, for pully to the organs, and shut-
    tynge the secounde belle rope . . . .   iij d.
To hym for hangynge the clothe before the rood in
    Lent, and iij°. cordes for the same . . .   iiij d.
Paid for fastenynge our Lady belle and the new belle in
    ther stockes . . . . iij s. iiij. d.
Paid for mendynge the wevers [2] sute of vestements,
    and a coope withe whyt lyos, and ij°. other coopis
    withe the flowerdeluce, to Thomas Rushberi .   vj d.
For the same, v. yeardes cheker las [3] . . . .   iij d.
In blacke thred and red . . . . . .   ij d.
Paid good wyffe Troyte, for ij. li. half wax for the holy
    candelle . . . . ij s. vj d.
And half a roope for the new belle . . . . ij s. iiij d.
Paid John Blount, for mendynge the wyndles in the
    stepulle at . . . .   xiiij d.
Paid for mendynge claper of our Lady belle, and the
    claper of the thrid belle, and the claper of the yeld [4]
    belle . . . . iij s. iiij d.

[1]. Dowlas, a sort of coarse linen imported from Britany.
[2] Perhaps the ceremonial dress of the wevers, mended now for some special occasion.
[3] cheker lace.   [4] i. e. Gild.

For mendynge gugyne,[1] and settynge upright the secound belle   xij d.

For a new bawdricke for our Lady belle   .   .   .   xviij d.

To make the pascalle, v. li. waxe at xij d.   .   .   v s.

To Humffry Belleman for his flees at the makynge the
    pascalle   .   .   .   .   iiij d.

Paid for mendynge the bere   .   .   .   .   iij d.

In nayles for the same bere   .   .   .   .   iij d.

In pyns and poyntes to dresse the canpie[2] to beare over
    the sacrament on Palme Sonday   .   .   .   ij d.

In great tackes to dresse the sepulcer .   .   .   iij d.

Payd for a fylle[3] of tymber for the gratt in the churche
    yeard at   .   .   .   .   x d.

Paid Stephen Knyght for ij. hynges for the same   .   viij d.

For shutynge[4] on of the old hynges   .   .   .   ij d.

And for nayles for the same gatt   .   .   .   iiij d.

Paid John Blunt for on borde, and mendynge the same gatt   xv d.

Paid Wryght the kerver, for mendynge the bere   .   iiij d.

Paid Rushebery for mendynge a coope of the gyst of
    m^r Foxe, and paralynge[5] the albes   .   .   .   ij d.

Paid John Blount for tymber and mendynge the bere   .   x d.

Paid Rusheberi the xviij. day of September to rynge
    curffur j li. of candelles at   .   .   .   .   ij d. ob.

A rope to the organs at   .   .   .   .   .   j d.

A lynke for visytynge at   .   .   .   .   .   x d.

In franke and sence   .   .   .   .   .   .   j d.

Paid Humfry Belleman for makynge clene the churche   ij s. viij d.

Paid John Smythe, baker, for carage of tymber out of
    Ludford to make the grate .   .   .   .   .   vj d.

And for carage of a lood stonys from the Friers[6] to the
    sayd grate .   .   .   .   .   .   iij d.

---

[1] The gudgeon was the large pivot of the axis of a wheel.   [2] The canopy.

[3] I am unacquainted with this term, which is probably a local word for a certain quantity.   [4] Fixing on.   [5] Perhaps for appareling.

[6] The Austin Friars, in Goalford, the ruins of which monastic house had at this time already become a great source of building and other materials.

And for carage of ij. loodes mouke [1] from under the gratt   vj d.

To John Raynoldes for iij. days woorke about the grate at   xviij d.

And to hym for carage of ramelle and stones from the
grate . . . . ij d.

Paid to John Alyan for pentynge the crosse clothe . vj s. viij d.

The xvj. day of November a pound of candels . . ij. d. ob.

To James Wylles to rynge day belle, a pound candels . ij d. ob.

Money more to hym to bye candles to rynge . . j d.

Paid to mr masson for a pes of tymber for the grate   vj s. viij d.

Paid to Perton for ij d. sawynge for the grate . . ij s. vj d.

Paid for j li. of candles for the furst masse . . . ij d. ob.

Paid for j. lode of tymber for the grate from Ludford   ij d.

Paid to Marten and Swyft, for iiij. dayes worke upon
the grate . . . . iij s. ij d.

Paid to Rawlens and Heynes for makynge clene the
grate hole . . . . vj d.

Paid mr Pooton, for a pece of tymber for a gutter
under the grate . . . . x d.

Paid to Powes, for a lynke to goo a vysettynge upon
our Lady day before Christmas . . . . x d.

Paid to Troyttes wyff the same day, for j. li. of syzes [2] . xij d.

Paid for ij. cordes for the organs . . . . ij d.

Paid to Wryght the joyner, for iij. deskes for the hyghe
chauncelle . . . . ij s. x d.

Paid for cordes to hange evy [3] and candelles upon at
Christmas . . . . vj d.

Paid to Troyttes wyff for d. j li. of syzes upon new
yers day . . . . vj d.

Paid for ij. li. of candles for the mydes of the churche
upon Christmas day . . . . . . v d.

Paid to Troyttes wyff for j. li. of syzes upon Sonday
after xij. day . . . . xij d.

---

[1] Muck.

[2] Sixes, as it is written in another place.   [3] *i. e.* ivy.

Paid to Thomas Wylson, to make clene on of the leades   ij d.

Paid to William Powes, for a lynke upon the Sounday
after Candelmas day, to goo a vysettynge   .   .   x d.

Paid for half a j. li. of frankeinsence and poynttes for
the canapie the same day   .   .   .   .   .   v d.

Paid to John Sothern, for iiij. bushelle of lyme to ley the
stones in saynt Johns chauncelle, over m^r Langfordes grave, and to mend the wyndow in our Lady
chauncelle and other places   .   .   .   xij d.

Paid to John Raynoldes, for fechynge of sande, and the
temperinge of the lyme and sande, and servynge the
pavyor of the same   .   .   .   .   .   vij d.

Paid to Thomas Season, for makynge the sepulcre, and
takynge downe the clothe over the roode, and pyns
and tackes .   .   .   .   xvj d.

Paid to John Blunt for the tymber of the sepulcre, and
his helpe to the makynge of the same   .   .   vj s.

Paid to Steven Knyght, for makynge of viij. rynges and
viij. staples and a hoke of yron for the sepulcre   .   xij d.

Paid to William Powes, for ij. lynkes at Ester to bere
before the sacrament   .   .   .   .   .   xx d.

Paid to William Powes, for a tapur for the sepulcur   .   vj d. ob.

Paid to Powes for makynge the pascalle   .   .   .   xj d.

Paid for a corde for the organs   .   .   .   .   j d.

Paid to Troyttes wyf for a lynke, that Rushebery sett to
goo a wyssettynge   .   .   .   .   .   viij d.

Paid for a chyme rope   .   .   .   .   .   ix. s. iiij d.

Paid for iij. half ropes at saynt Laurence fayer [1] for
the belles .   .   .   .   vj s. viij d.

Paid to Thomas a Crew for ij. bawdrykss for the great
belle, and mendynge of an old bawdryke   .   .   ij s. viij d.

---

[1] A fair was perhaps held on the day of St. Lawrence, the patron of the Church, the
dues, &c. of which went to the Church.

Paid to Humfrey the belman, for blowynge the organs   ij s. viij d.
Paid for j. li. of candles delyvered to ser Richard Cu-
per for the fyrst masse . . . . . .   ij d. ob.
Paid for j. li. of candles delyvered to James Wylles for
day belle . . . .   ij d. ob.
Paid for j li. of candles delyvered to the basse for the
furst masse . . . .   ij d. ob.
Paid to Troyttes wyf for half j. li. of waxe syzes . .   vij d.
Paid for candles delyvered to James Wyles to rynge
day belle . . . .   j d.
Paid for candles for Lygan at the stokynge[1] of the belle   j d.
j. elle of fyne Holland for the crosse clothe . .   xxiij d.
Paid for a sensor and a ship,[2] to m^r Masson . .   xxj s.

Summa vij li. iij s. iiij d.

Receyttes of money by us the forsayd churche wardens.

Receyved at Ester for the parte of money payd at the
receyvinge of the sacrament . . . .   xl s.
Received of m^r Whytlege for the beryalle of a straunge
man in the churche . . . . .   vj s. viij d.
Received of m^r Wheliex for the berialle of his wif . vj s. viij d.
Received of m^r Taylor for the berialle of his wif . . vj s. viij d.
Received of m^r Cox for the berialle of his doughter . vj s. viij d.
Received of m^r Alsope for the berialle of his wife   vj s. viij d.
Received for a pewe in the lower end of the churche
set to Richard Rascalle and Edmund Hountte .   vj s.
Received for the ground of a pewe before saynt Johns
chauncelle set to Resse ap Thomas . . .   xiiij d.
Received of William Bedow for the olde rope of the chymes   ij s. iiij d.

[1] Fixing.
[2] The vessel in which the frankincense was kept, and which in the medieval Church was made in the form of a ship. Ducange, under the word *Navis*, quotes the will of a bishop of Beauvais, dated in 1217, who left to his cathedral, among other things, "calicem unum aureum, et *narem* argenteam, et missale."

Received for a pewe behynde the northe dore set to William
    Parteryge Walker .   .   .   .   .   ij s. viij d.

Received for a parte in a pewe behynde the sayd northe
    dore set to Henry Jonys .   .   .   .   xij d.

Received for the grounde of a pewe before the southe
    dore to Thomas Hount and Saunders Willyams[1]   ij s. viij d.

Received of Rychard Langham for a lyttelle pewe behynde
    the sayd northe dore .   .   .   .   .   xij d.

Received for getherynge of the quarterege boke in money xxxv s. xd.

           Summa . . vj li. vj s.

Received more of m^r Langford, for iiij. peces of tymber .   xij d.

Received for a parte in a pewe in the lower end of the
    churche next to the place of saynt Stevens chaun-
    celle, to John Rawlyns .   .   .   .   ii s. viij d.

Item, the churche wardens most receave of m^r Sher-
    mond for the bryke closse²   .   .   .   viij s.

So that the parishe restithe in the churche wardens dette v s. viij d.

For the whiche some of v s. viij d. m^r baylifes hathe
    graunted the sayd churche wardens a pewe at the
    nether yende³ of the churche, one the right hand
    the wedynge dore late in the tenure of m^{res} Hud-
    son, payinge unto the new churche wardens, over
    the same some of v s. viij d.   . .   iij s.

        ffinis.

The accomptes of suche charges as we, Robert Lewys and
    Rychard Rascolle, beynge electyd churche wardens
    in the yeare of our Lord 1555, have ben charged in
    the tyme of our offyce untylle the feast of Symon and
    Jude thappostelles, then next ensuyeng, viz. 1556.

In primis delyvered to James Wylles j. li. of candles, to
    rynge day belle withe .   .   .   .   .   ij d. ob.

---

    ¹ These last three words are added in a different hand.
    ² This " brick close" is not unfrequently mentioned in the course of these Accounts,
but its exact position is not described.   ³ end.

Item, delyvered to Rushberi j li. of candles to rynge curfur
with . . . . ij d. ob.

Paid for a cord to the organs . . . . . j d.

Delyvered to ser Rychard Cowper, ij li. of candles for
the fyrst masse and for the lampe . . . v d.

Paid to Johan Troyte, for j li. of waxe that was delyvered in the tyme of Thomas Blackbacche and
Thomas Bedo . . . . ix d.

Item, paid to the sayd Johan, for j li. and dim. of waxe,
that was delyvered in the tyme of Laurens Becke
and Rychard Farre . . . . . . xviij d.

Paid to Phelyp tynker for mendynge a censor and the
fote of the holy water potte . . . . vj d.

Paid to Rychard Swanse, for a rope to the fyrst mas
belle . . . . xvij d.

Paid to Thomas Season and to John Blont and hys man
for a dayes worke and dim. in the hangynge of ij.
belles in the steple . . . . . . iij s. iiij d.

Paid to Crosse for the mendynge of a gogyng [1] to the
fore belle . . . . iiij d.

Paid to the sayd Crosse, for nayles and the settynge on
of the locke of the sowthe dore . . . ij d.

To the sayd Crosse for mendynge the locke of the wed-
dyng dore . . . . ij d.

Item, to Crosse for the locke and the key of the northe
dore . . . . ij s.

Item, to Crosse for a locke to the steple dore . . vj d.

Item, to Crosse for a key and nayles to the vestry dore xiiij d.

Item, for a hocke [2] that was made for the gable of the
castylle . . . . xij d.

Paid to Rychard Swanse for ij. ropes, one for the fore
belle, and the other for the secound belle . . iiij s. x d.

[1] The gudgeon was the large pivot of the axle of a wheel.
[2] A hook.

Paid to the sayd Rychard for nayles and for the naylynge of the cover of the font .   .   .   .   j d.

Paid for a corde to the organs in the lofte .   .   j d.

Delyvered to the pavyer ij li. of candles for Christmas
   day in the mornynge   .   .   .   .   v d.

Paid to the sayd pavyer toward the coordes and the yvyc
   at Christmas .   .   .   .   .   .   iiij d.

Paid to Johan Troyte for a lynke of 3 li. 3 quarters
   for to vysete withalle .   .   .   .   xviij d.

Paid to the sayd Johan for j. li. of syses agaynst Christmas   xij d.

Delyvered to Rusbery j li. of candles for curfur .   ij d. ob.

To the sayd Rusbery of frankeinsence   .   .   j d.

Paid for the berynge of the gable ropes and the pullese [1]
   into the castle .   .   .   .   .   ij d.

Delyvered to ser Rychard Cupper and to ser Thomas
   Charme ij li. of candles for the fyrst mase and the lampe   vj d.

Paid to Walter Whyte for wryttynge the booke of the
   paryshyoners names .   .   .   .   ij d.

Delyvered to Rusbery j. li. of candles .   .   .   iiij d.

Paid to Crosse for iiij. plates to the fore belle .   ij d.

Paid to John Dowghton for the bendynge [2] of a prycke
   songe booke .   .   .   .   .   iiij s.

Paid to Johan Troyte for iiij. li. of waxe and for the
   makynge of the same for the holy candle .   iiij s.

Paid to the sayd Johan for j. li. of syses and for a whope[3]
   of charcoles .   .   .   .   xv d.

Paid to Rychard Farre for ij. ellys and a half of dowles[4]
   to make Rusbery a syrples .   .   .   iiij s.

Paid to Marget Newalle, for the makynge of the same .   vij d.

Paid to Phelyp tynker for the mendynge of the corps belle   xij d.

Paid to Rusbery for a lynke .   .   .   xij d.

---

[1] pulleys.

[2] binding, which appears to have been expensive at this time ; or this book must have been very richly bound.

[3] Probably some local name for a measure of charcoals.   [4] Dowlas, see before. p. 15.

Delivered to Rusbery j. li. of candles for curfur   .   .   iij d.

Delivered to Rychard Cupper in candles for the fyrst masse   j d.

Paid to Thomas Season for glasynge of viij. fote in
saynt Mergetes wyndow   .   .   .   iiij s. viij d.

Paid for lyme to set up the sayd pane   .   .   j d.

Paid to the sayd Thomas for the shuttynge of iiij. of
the belle roopes . . . . viij d.

Paid to the sayd Thomas for puttynge the corde of the
lampe into the tryselle   .   .   .   . ij d.

Paid to Crosse for mendynge the locke and makynge a
bolt of saynt Johns chapelle dore   .   .   . iiij d.

Paid to Thomas Season for hangynge the clothe before
the roode . . . . iiij d.

Paid for cordes and packethrede for the sayd clothe
agaynst Palmsonday . . . . . viij d. ob.

Paid to the sayd Thomas for hangynge the loker and
fastnynge the coordes to draw up the clothe .   . ij d.

Paid for iij. lode of lyme . . . . . xviij d.

Paid to Thomas Dyke and Lewys Gwyn for ij. days worke
and a halfe in swepynge the walles of the churche and
whytlymynge the porche   .   .   .   . iij s. v d.

Paid for pyns, poyntes, and packethrede, for the canapie
upon Palmsondaye   .   .   .   .   . j d. ob.

Paid to Thomas Turner for mendynge the pascalle stocke   iij d.

Paid to Rychard Farre for x li. of waxe to make the
pascalle . . . . ix s. ij d.

Paid to Johan Troyte for makynge the pascalle .   . xvj d.

Paid to the pavyer for his fees   .   .   .   . iiij d.

Paid for half a pound of frankincense   .   . iiij d.

Paid for rosen agaynst Ester   .   .   . ob.

Paid for a bushelle of charcoles [1]   .   .   . iiij. d.

---

[1] This is I think the first of these Accounts in which the word charcoals is used, and
it would seem to show that the use of mineral coals was becoming more common. *Char-*
coal is found as the interpretation of *carbo* in the Promptorium Parvulorum, the English-
Latin dictionary of the middle of the fifteenth century.

Paid for ij. tapers of j. li. for the sepulcre . . . xij d.

Paid to John the laborer for mendynge the rayle of the
 steyr of the clocke house . . . . j d.

Paid to John Newton for skowrynge the plate of the
 crosse staf and settynge the same upon a staffe that
 the sayd John gave to the paryshe . . . iiij d.

Paid to Walter Bold for makynge the holy water stoone iiij s. iiij d.

Paid to John Smythe for karyenge the sayd stone to
 the churche . . . . . . iiij d.

Paid to Rusbery towardes a breckfast for the ryngers of
 day belle . . . . xij d.

Item, in pyns and in whypcorde for the sepulcure . ij d. ob.

Paid to Thomas Season for shuttynge the rope of the
 fore belle . . . . ij d.

Paid to the sayd Thomas for dressynge of the sepulcre xij d.

Item, to William Benson for j. c. of tackes to the sepulcur ij d.

Paid to Thomas Turner for mendynge the bere . . ij d.

Paid for 3 burthen of roodes[1] to wynde the wals of
 the store howse . . . . . . vj d.

Paid to Johan the laborer for comynge and wyndynge
 of the sayd walles . . . . . iiij d.

Paid to Thomas Season for v. li. of sowder to sowder
 the leades of the churche . . . . ij s. vj d.

Payd to Margery Davys for the karyage of the mucke
 owt of the churche yearde that was throwen owt of
 the leades . . . . ij d.

Paid for woode and cooles that sowdryde the leades . iiij d.

Paid for rosen to the sayd leades . . . . ob.

Paid to Crosse for makynge a staple to the thyrde belle iij d.

Paid to Rusbery for the mendynge of the wevers vestment and for ij. coopes of red velvet . . . iiij d. ob.

Paid for pyns and poyntes for the canape agaynst Corpus
 Christi tyde . . . . . . j d.

_____
[1] laths.

Paid for a corde to the organs . . . . . j d.

Paid to Wylliam Beado for a borde to make the crosse
dore in the churchyarde . . . . . xj d.

Paid to Gryffethe for ij. ledges and for the makynge of
the dore . . . . vj d.

Item, for nayles to the saide dore . . . . j d. ob.

Paid to Crosse for the makynge of a bokle to the bal-
dryke of the secounde belle . . . . ij d.

Paid for ij. halters for the organs . . . . ij d.

Paid for ij. lynkes that we helde by the pascalle upon Ester
day in the mornynge . . . . . . xx d.

Paid to Season for mendynge the balyse [1] of the organs ij d.

Paid to the sayde Season for glasynge of iiij. fote in saynt
Katerynes wyndow . . . . . . ij s. viij d.

Paid for lyme to set up the sayde glasse . . . j d.

Paid for the makynge clene of the steyres of the steple iiij d.

Paid to John Dawghton, for the bendynge of iiij. Proces-
sionales and for the mendynge of one Antyphonar [2] iij s. viij d.

Delyvered to John Broke in paper ryalle . . . ij d.

Paid the pavier his fees for makynge clene the churche
and for the organs . . . . . . v s. viij d.

Paid for ij. hookes to hange the churchyarde dore . ij d.

Paid for a lynke of iij. li. iij. quarters . . . . xviij d.

Paid to Thomas Season for a loker to the great belle
and for shuttynge the rope of the secounde belle . iiij d.

Paid to the sayd Thomas for mendynge the candelstycke
of the hyghe alter . . . . . . iiij d.

Paid to the sayd Thomas for a borde that mendyde the
wheles of our Lady belle and the secounde tenor ij s.

Paid for nayles that mendede the sayd wheles . ij d.

Paid for mendynge the sayde wheles . . . . v d.

Delyvered to James Wylles in candles to rynge day belle with j d.

[1] Bellows.

[2] These were of course two of the important books of the Popish service, the Proces-
sional and the Antiphonary.

Delyvered to Rusbery in candles to rynge curfur   .   iij d.

Item, in candles to James Wylles to rynge day belle   .   iij d.

Paid to Thomas a Crew for the mendynge of the baw-
    dryke to the thyrde belle   .   .   .   .   .   iiij d.

Item, in candles to Rushbery for curfur   .   .   .   iij d.

Delivered to ser Thomas Charme and ser Rycharde
    Cupper ij. li. of candles for the first masse and
    the lampe .   .   .   .   vj. ob.

Paid for dyggynge and syftynge of iiij. loode of sande
    for the steple   .   .   .   .   viij d.

Paid to John Smythe for the karyage of the sayde iij.
    loodes   .   .   .   .   xviij d.

Item, for the karyage of the sayde sande into the steple   xx d.

Item, for the makynge cleane of saynt Johns leades, and
    of the steple leades, and for the karyage away of the
    same   .   .   .   .   iiij d.

Paid, to Phelyp tynker for x. li. of sowder to sowdre the
    leades of the steple   .   .   .   .   .   .   v s.

Paid for woode to melt the sowdre   .   .   .   .   iiij d.

Item, for rosen and talow for the leades   .   .   .   ij d.

Paid for iij. c. and x. li. nayles to William Benson for
    the leades .   .   .   .   xx d.

Paid to a workeman that attendede upon Phelyp tynker,
    and also that karyede the leade out of the steple .   vj d.

Paid to Phelyp for leynge the leades of the steple   xxvj s. viij d.

Paid to Johan Troyte for a lynke of j. li. qr.   .   .   vj d.

Paid for a rope for the great belle   .   .   .   .   ij s. vj d.

Item, to Richarde Farre, for two unces of frankeincense   iiij d.

Paid to Thomas Season for shuttynge the rope of our
    Lady belle   .   .   .   .   ij d.

Paid to Johan Troyte for ij. cordes for the organs   .   ij d.

Paid to the sayde Johane for half a pounde of syses agaynst
    Halowtyde   .   .   .   .   vij d.

Payd to James Wylles in candles to rynge day belle   .   j d.

Paid to Margery Pyrne for iiij. yeardes and dim. of heere
    clothe [1] for the hyghe alter . . . . .   iij s. ij d.
Paid to Rushbery for the sowynge of the sayd heere clothe   j d.
Paid to the sayd Rushbery for thapparelynge of a dor-
    nyx albe[2]. . . . . . .   j d.
Paid to m^r Person, for kepynge the parishe boke
Delivered to the pavyer a corde for the baylise of the organs   j d.
          Summa . vij li. iiij s. ob.

The accomptes of the receytes that we the sayd churche
wardens have recevyd for the churche within the
tyme of our offyce.

In primis, of William Beado for the grave of a con-
    demnyd man . . . .   viij d.
Item, of the parishe at Ester . . . .   xxxvj s. ix d.
Item, for the graves of m^r Lokyer and his wyff .   xiij s. iiij d.
Item, for the grave of Walter Brocton . . .   vj s. viij d.
Item, for the grave of William Parteryge . .   vj s. viij d.
Item, for the grave of William Clere . . .   vj s. viij d.
Item, of Laurens Becke and Rychard Farre for a pewe
    in the west end of the churche, late in the hold
    of Margett Hodson . . . . . .   iij s.
Item, of Robert Strynger and Walter Jones, for a pew
    in the northe syde of the churche, late in the hold
    of m^r Lokyer . . . .   vij s. ij d.
Item, of Robert Lewys and Rychard Rascolle, for a pew
    in the west end of the churche, late in the hold of
    m^{rs} Calfyld . . . . .   vj s. viij d.

---

[1] Hair-cloth.

[2] Dornik, or Doornick, is the Flemish name for the town which the French and English call Tournay, where formerly a flourishing trade was carried on in linen manufac-
tured there. The alb here mentioned was no doubt made of Tournay linen. At this
time, for several reasons, an extensive trade was carried on between our country and
Flanders.

Item, for as moche as m^r Mason hathe bowght of m^r
    Cother the interest of his pew over agaynst the
    pulpit, we have sett to the sayd m^r Mason the sayd
    pew, in satisfaccion whereof the sayd m^r Mason
    hath surrenderyd unto the paryshe hys interest in
    the pew withe Thomas Beado.

Item, of the paryshnors, as yt apperythe by the quarter-
    yge boke   .   .   .   .   lj s. v d.

Item, received of Thomas Beado for the interest that
    m^r Mason had in his pew   .   .   .   .   .   iij s. iiij d.

Item, of John Season for a pew in the mydle of the
    churche late in the hold of Willyam Parteryche
    thelder   .   .   .   .   xx d.

Summa of recettes   .   .   vij li. iiij s.

So the churche restithe in the churche wardens dett   0 ob.
                                ffinis.

Reparacions done upon the churche and other necessary
    charges therunto belonginge, disbursed and payd
    by Richard Pooton and Rychard Tomlyns, churche
    wardens ffrom the ffeast of alle seyntes in anno
    Domini 1556, for and in the tyme of one whole yere
    then next ensuynge, viz. unto the seid feaste anno
    Domini 1557.

In primis, payd to Thomas Rusheburie for syse to rynge
    corfur from the tyme of our entrye in to our office
    untille Candlemas   .   .   .   .   .   .   ix d.

Item, to James Rigmayne for syse to rynge daybelle
    durynge the said tyme   .   .   .   .   .   ix d.

Item, to ser [1] Thomas Chyrme for a pound of tallow
    candles to say the furst masse   .   .   .   .   iij d. ob.

---

[1] It may be perhaps well to remark that *ser*, or *sir* representing the Latin *dominus*, was the usual title of a priest, or of any one who had taken his first university degree.

Item, to ser Rychard Cuper for another pound of candles
to the same use . . . . . . iij d. ob.
Item, to the sayd ser Richard for a pound of smale tallow candells for the lampe in the myddle of the
churche . . . . iij d. ob.
Item, to William Powis for a pound of sise for the quere
at mattens and evensonge . . . . . vj d.
Item, to Agnes Troyte, wido, for another half pound of
syse to the same use . . . . . . vj d.
Item, to William Powis for a lynke of iij li. and a half,
delyvered unto ser Thomas Chyrme to burne at
the elevacon of the sacrament at the furst masse xij d.
Item, to the sayd William Powis for another lynke
delyvered to ser Richard Cupper to the same use
of ij poundes and a half . . . . . viij d.
Item, Thomas Season for iij. triselles for the great organs ij d.
Item, to Antony Atkynson for ij. poundes of wyre to
amende the chymes . . . . . . xvj d.
Item, to Thomas Season and Thomas Rushburie for
amendynge the sayd chymes . . . . xiij s. iiij d.
Item, to the sayd Season for a pere of cruettes of tyne
for the highe chauncelle . . . . . xij d.
Item, to the sayd Season for a locker to the gret belle . ij d.
Item, to Stephen Knyght for a longe stalke of iron of iij.
fote to amende one of the hammers of the chymes
and makynge a clyp of iron to blase the sacringe
belle of a fote and a half longe and a pyne of iron of
a fote longe for the chymes and iij. gret nayles for
the same belle and amendynge the same . . xviij d.
Item, to William Powis for another half a pound of syse
for the quere . . . . vj d.
Item, to ser Thomas, another pound of tallow candles
for the furst masse . . . . . . iij d. ob.

Item, to Agnes Troyte, for a lynke of a pound and a
half to visett withe . . . . . . ix d.

Item, to Thomas Dyke and Leawys Gwyn, for a days
worke a pece in swepynge the churche walles
agaynst Christmas . . . . . . xx d.

Item, to the pavier for ij. pounde of tallow candles for
the churche at Christmas . . . . . vij d.

Item, to the sayd pavier to bye hollye and evye agaynst
the same tyme . . . . iiij d.

Item, to William Powis for a pound and half of syse
agaynst the same tyme . . . . . xviij d.

Item, to hym for a lynke of iij. li. and iij. quarters to
lyght at after evensonge, to synge carolles at the
same tyme . . . . xij d.

Item, to Thomas Ffranke for ij. cordes to the organs . ij d.

Item, for a quarter of frankensence . . . . ij d.

Item, for charke cooles [1] . . . . . . iiij d.

Item, for one rent bord to amend the bere . . ij d.

Item, to Roger Swylte for amendynge the same bere . ij d.

Item, for borde nayle [2] to amend the same bere . . j d.

Item, to William Powis and Agnes Troyte for a pound
of syse . . . . xij d.

Item, to the sayd Agnes Troyte for a lynke of iiij.
poundes to visett withe alle . . . . . xviij d.

Item, to Thomas a Crew for a baldrope for the secounde
belle . . . . xx d.

Item, to Thomas Season for hanginge up the sacringe
belle and puttynge the same into the olde stocke . vj d.

Item, to the sayd Thomas for shuttynge ij. olde belle ropes ij d.

Item, for a rope for the chymes of xl. fteadome,[3] and
another rope for the same use of xv. fteadome . viijs. ix d.

---

[1] Charcoals. [2] Board-nails.

[3] Forty fathoms. It appears that ropes of great magnitude were fetched from Worcester.

Item, for the cariage of the same from Worceter to this
towne . . . . xij d.

Item, to John Broke for paper to pricke songes for the
churche . . . . ij d.

Item, to Philip tynker for mendynge the lampe in the
highe chauncelle . . . . . . xij d.

Item, to Thomas Season and Thomas Rushburie for
hanginge up the same in his olde place . . ij d.

Item, to William Powis for a corde of viij. ffedome to
hange up the same . . . . . . viij d.

Item, to the sayd William Powis for a lynke to visett
with alle . . . . xiiij d.

Item, for ij. pounde and an halfe of waxe to make the holy
candle at Candelmas . . . . . . ij s. vj d.

Item, to Stephen Knyght for mendynge the goodgyn[1]
of the secounde belle . . . . . . ij d.

Item, to Thomas Season, Rushburie, and Humfry Season, for ther labors in remucinge the saide belle, and
amendynge the brasse about bothe goodgynes . vj d.

Item, to the said Thomas Season for amendynge the
sencer . . . . ij d.

Item, to William Powis for a lynke of iij. li. to visitt
with alle . . . . xij d.

Item, for pynnes and poyntes upon Palme Sondaye, to
tye up the coverelett in the churche over the off-
ringe place . . . . ij d.

Item, for tacke nayle and borde nayle for the sepulcre,
to Rychard Kerver . . . . . . v d.

Item, for pynes for the same . . . . . j d.

Item, for whipcoord to draw the curten of the same . ij d.

Item, to Rusheburie for a pound of tallow candles. . iij d. ob.

Item, for nayles for the Judas crosse . . . . j d.

---

[1] The gudgeon. See before, p. 67.

Item, for a pece of tymber and mendynge the same,
to Thomas Turnor . . . . . . ij d.
Item, to Agnes Troyte, for a lynke of ij. pounde and
half to visitt with alle . . . . . . x d.
Item, for 8 bz. of charke coole agaynst Easter . iiij d.
Item, to Richard Season for makynge clene the stayres
of the steple . . . . j d.
Item, to William Powis for a quarter of syse afore
Easter . . . . iij d.
Item, to Thomas Season for hanginge the clothe over
the roode upon Palme Sonday, and the locker for
drawinge the same . , ... vj d.
Item, to hym for iij dayes worke in settynge up the
sepulcre . . . . xviij d.
Item, to hym for makynge and kervinge the image for
the resurrexcion . . . . . . xviij d.
Item, the pavier for his ffees . . . . . iiij d.
Item, to Rushburie for makynge a brekfaste to those
that rynge daybelle in the Easter weke . . xij d.
Item, to William Powis for syse againste Easter . j d.
Item, for iiij. pounde of waxe to William Powis towardes
the makynge of the pascalle . . . . iiij s. viij d.
Item, to Hew Taylor for vij. poundes of waxe for the
same use . . . . viij s. ix d.
Item, to William Powis for makynge the same after
the rate of j. d. the pounde. . . . . xj d.
Item, to hym for ij. lyttle tapers for the sepulcre . ij d.
Item, to hym for makynge the toppe of one of them
anewe after hit was burnt out in the sepulcre . j d.
Item, for ij. lynkes to the said Powis agaynst Easter . xx d.
Item, for half a pounde of rosen . . . . j d.
Item, for a quarter of a pounde of waxe to closse the
stocke to William Powis . . . . . iiij d. ob.

Item, to James Willes for iiij. burden of roddes [1] for the
house in the church yearde . . . . . viij d.

Item, to John of Dynham, for ij. burden to the same
use . . . . iiij d.

Item, for stedes to put in the wales ⌐. . . . j d.

Item, for nayles . . . . j d.

Item, to William Powis for a lynke of ij. poundes and
half to visitt withe . . . . . . x d.

Item, to John Smythe, for iij. lode of cleye for the
church house . . . . xij d.

Item, to x. bushelles of lyme to plaster the same house ij s. vj d.

Item, to Thomas Willson, for iiij. dayes worke in wyndynge, plastringe, and whitlymynge the said house ij s. iiij d.

Item, to John Hannse for reparinge and makynge a
newe of ij. olde pewes at the northe dore, a daye . viij d.

Item, to Anne of the Cornelle, for swepinge and makynge cleane alle the nether parte of the churche . ij d.

Item, to Rycharde Kerver for nayles to amende the same ij d.

Item, for bordes and nayles, tymber for the same, to the
said Hannee . . . . . . xx d.

Item, to Thomas a Crew for mendynge the baldrop [2] of
the secounde belle . . . . . iiij d.

Item, to hym for mendynge the baldrope of the first
belle . . . . iiij d.

Item, to Thomas Season for mendyng the candlestycke
of the highe alter . . . . . . vj d.

Item, to hym for knittinge iij. belle ropes . . . ij d.

Item, to William Powis for a lynke of ij. pounde and a
half . . . . x d.

Item, to Thomas Ffranke for iiij. cordes for the organs iiij d.

[1] **Laths.** They were used apparently for repairing or enlarging the timber house in the churchyard, which appears to have been done to a considerable extent in this year.

[2] Another form of baldrick.

Item, to John Rawlyns for mendynge the baldrope of
 the Lady belle . . . . . viij d.
Item, to Stephen Knyght for makynge a new baldropez
 buccle for the sayd belle . . . . . ij d.
Item, to hym for makynge the brastes [1] and other iron
 worke for the great belle, and for xxxj. nayles for
 the same . . . . iij s.
Item, to Thomas Season for iij. fote of glasse and half,
 and the leede, and sowder for the same, and puttinge the same in saynt Mergarettes chauncelle
 window . . . . ij s. iiij d.
Item, for mendynge of a pane of glasse to hym in the
 southe yle, and leede and sowder . . . vj d.
Item, for a fotte of new glasse to amende the same pane,
 and lede and sowder . . . . . . viij d.
Item, for swaile for a saunce belle [2] . . . ij d.
Item, for shotinge the roopes of the gret belle and seconde
 tenor . . . . iiij d.
Item, for vj. ringes for the organs to the seid Season,
 and sowinge them withe amblettes [3] . . . vj d.
Item, to Stephen Knight for ij. hokes and a staple for the
 churche yearde gate . . . . . vj d.
Item, to John Blunte for xx. rent boordes to amende the
 windowes in the steple . . . . vj s.
Item, to hym for iiij dayes worke there, and amendinge
 the dore goinge to the colledge, after x d. the daye iij s. iiij d.
Item, to one laborer withe hym iiij. dayes . . . ij s.
Item, to another ij. dayes. . . . . xvj d.
Item, to the sayde Blunt for a longe planke . . xij d.
Item, to hym for a lader to go out of the belle house
 downe to the chymes . . . . . viij d.

[1] A word I have not met with elsewhere, nor do I know its meaning.— *Braces ?*
[2] The saints' bell, or small bell which called to religious services.
[3] Also a word I have not previously met with.

Item, to hym for ij. peces of tymber to amende the sayde
dore . . . .   iij d.

Item, to Robert Mason for xv. sawede boordes to <u>slore</u> [1]
the seconde lofte in the steple . . . .   xv s.

Item, to Richard Kerver, for nayles for to nayle the
same, and the boordes in the sayd windowes .   xij d.

Item, to William Merteyne and John Blunte, for a dayes
worke a pese in mendynge the grett belle .   xxij d.

Item, to iij. laborers withe them the same daye . .   ij s.

Item, to William Powis for half a belle rope for the gret
belle . . . .   ij s. viij d.

Item, to Richard Crosse, for mendynge the locke of the
vestrye dore, and makynge a newe keye to the
same, and for iiij. gret new nayles . . .   xvj d.

Item, to Walter Bolde, for a dayes worke in settynge in
the tablettes of leede in the walles over the northe
side of the churche, and plasteringe the same, and
for his man . . . .   ij s.

Item, to Rusheburie, for a pounde of candles to rynge
curfur . . . .   iij d.

Item, to James Willes for another pounde of candles to
rynge daye belle . . . . . .   iij d.

Item, to ser Thomas Cherme and ser Richarde Cupper,
for a pounde of candles to saye the first masse .   iij d.

Item, to William Powis, for a lynke of ij. poundes and
half, to visett withe . . . . .   x d.

Item, to hym for a li. of syse against Allhallontide [2] .   xij d.

Item, to Andrew Sonybanke, for iij. ounces of silver
for the fote of the grett chalice, after v s. the ounce   xv s.

Item, to the seid Andrew, ffor an olde angelle [3] and half
to gilde the same . . . . . .   xvj s. vj d.

---

[1] This means apparently to cover or strengthen the second floor, but I have not met
with the word elsewhere.   [2] All Saints' day.

[3] An angel was a gold coin of the value of 6s. 8d. (which became a lawyer's fee), but an
old angel appears at this time to have been of considerably more value.

Item, to hym for workinge of the same, beinge x^{en}
 ounces after the rate of x^d. the ounce . . . viij s. iiijd.
Item, to William Powis, for ij. linkes of iij. poundes a
 pese to visett withe . . . . . ij s.
Item, to Richarde Swanseye, for half a belle rope for the
 secounde belle . . . . . . ij s. j d.
Item, to the pavier for his ffees for makynge clene the
 churche and blowinge the organs . . . v s. iiij d.
   Summa . ix li. xj s. iij d.

Receyved the said yere by us, Richard Pooton and
 Richard Tomlyns, churche wardens, to the use of
 the parishe, towardes the reparacons of the same
 churche, and other necessarye charges therunto belonginge, the particuler summs of money subscribed.

In primis, received of John Buston, for his quarterage,
 unpaid alle the last yere, towardes the reparacons of
 the churche . . . . iiij d.
Item, of m^r Wheler, for his late wifes grave in the
 churche . . . . vj s. viij d.
Item, of Mores Philipes, for the like for his late wif . vj s. viij d.
Item, at Easter of houslinge people[1] . . . xxxiij s. iiij d.
Item, of m^{es} Bradforde, for her late husbandes grave
 in the churche . . . . . . vj s. viij d.
Item, of Richard Blashefilde, for his ffathers grave in the
 same churche . . . . . . vj s. viij d.

---

[1] Communicants. To *housele*, in old English, meant, to administer the sacrament. The word in **Anglo-Saxon** was *huslian*, to make the offering, and *husel*, or *husol*, meant the offering of the sacrament.

Item, of the inhabitantes for ther quarterages for the
    whole yere . . . . lij s. j d.
Item, of John Shermond, for his mothers grave in the
    churche. . . . . v s. viij d.
Item, of our m^{rs} of the vj. men for the amendynge
    of the grett chalice, and the gildinge of the same,
    withe the workemanship of the goldsmythe . . xl s.
        Summa . . viij li. viij d.

Memorandum, that we Richard Pooton and Richard
Tomlyns, churche wardens, have graunted, withe the
consent of m^r bailifes the seid yere, the pewis under
written unto the persons subscribed for the somes
of money upon ther names apperinge.

In primis, graunted and sett unto Mergett Ockley, the
    iij^d parte of a pewe at the nether ende of the
    churche, withe good wife Sharwleye and good wif
    Troyte, for . . . . xviij d.
Item, to Edmonde Cother, for his late mothers pewe at
    the nether ende of the said churche . . . iij s. iiij d.
Item, to Walter Bolde, a olde pewe at the northe dore
    for . . . . xx d.
Item, to m^{es} Partriche, widow, the iiij. parte of a
    pewe with Hary Jonys wif and others, at the said
    northe doore for . . . . . . xij d.
Item, to William Pike, for a pew at the southe dore,
    late Peter Ffourdes . . . . . . ij s.
Item, to John Bottfilde and John Taylor, penter, for a
    new pewe at the northe dore . . . . iij s. iiij d.

deuyed
upon
considera-
con.

{ Item, to John Shermonde, for iij. pewes, late
Edmunde Shermonde his father, wherof
one at the weddinge doore, another behind
the northe dore, and the other on the
northe yle, ageinst the pullpitt; after the
rate of iij s. iiij d. a pese[1]   .   .   .   x s.

Item, to Richard Tomlyns, a pew late John Gwynis
wifes father decessed   .   .   .   .   .   .   ij s.

Item, to William Philipes the yonger, one pew, surrendred to the churche by Robert Mason, and
late in the tenure of Thomas Cother   .   .   .   xij d.

Summa   .   .   xv s. x d.
ffinis.

So the churche owith the churche wardens 0.

Memorandum, leyd out and paid by me, Richard Blasfild
and William Bradshalle, churche wardens, in anno
Domini 1557, and endede of the same in anno Domini 1558.

Item, paid to James Willes for candles to rynge day belle   viij d.
Paid for nayles to mend the secounde belle   .   .   .   j d.
Paid for nayles to fastene the stocke of the same belle   .   iiij d.
Paid for candles for the ij. pristes to singe the first mase   vj d.
Paid to Rushebery for candles   .   .   .   .   .   iij d.
Paid for clystes to make[2] handes .   .   .   .   .   vj d.
Paid for tymber to fasten the iij. whelles[3]   .   .   .   iij d.
Paid to Mitten and his man for iij. dayes workeinge
upon the lokers and the handes .   .   .   .   v s. iij d.

[1] This item is cancelled in the original.
[2] I suppose that the word *hands* means here, handles; and that *clystes* were some materials used for making them.   In old French the word *clister* meant, to cover with rags.
[3] Wheels.

Paid to Thomas Season for glassinge the churche . iij s. iiij d.

Paid for a baudrycke for the secounde tenor . . ij s. ij d.

Paid for nayles and ij. piecs yeorne [1] for the secounde belle viij d.

Paid for candles to the belle man to serve at Christmas vij d.

Paid for ij. li. of sysses to William Powis . . . ij s.

Paid for ij. lynkes for the quier . . . . . xx d.

Paid for ij. pounde of candles d. ser Rychard Cupper
for first mase . . . . vij d.

Paid Rusbery for j. pound of candles . . . iij d. ob.

Paid for cordes to the organs . . . . ij d.

Paid for one burelle [2] of colles . . . ij d.

Paid for a lynke to Johan Troyte . . . . x d.

Paid for frankensens . · . . . . iij d.

Paid for j. li. candles d. ser Rycharde Cupper . iij d.

Paid for j. li. candles d. Rusberi . . . . iij d.

Paid for woode . . . . . . iiij d.

Paid Richard Smythe for ij. dayes worke with Thomas
Season . . . . xiiij d.

Paid Thomas Season for iiij. li. of sowder . . . ij s.

Paid William Powis for ij. li. d. of holye candles and a
li. sysses . . . . iij s.

Paid for a launterne to visett withe alle . . . xvj d.

Paid to Thomas Season and to T. Dicke for pargettynge
of the hether side [3] of the churche . . . xviij d.

Paid to William Powis for xiij. li. of waxe to make the
pascalle . . . . xiij s.

Paid to him for a lynke . . . . . . viij d.

Paid Thomas Season for mendynge of the ij. wheles . vj d·

Paid him for mendynge the sepulcre . . . ij s.

Paid Watter Rosse for bokes to serve the churche . ij s.

Paid to Rusbery for j. pounde of candles . . . iij d.

---

[1] Pieces of iron.

[2] Apparently the, perhaps local, name of some measure of quantity.

[3] The hither side, or side towards the town.

Paid Thomas Season for makynge a barrelle to the organs
and coverynge the roude [1]   .   .   .   .   xij d.

Paid to the belle man for his quarterege   .   .   .   xvj d.

Paid to John of Dinaham [2] for his vj. dais worke . .   iij s.

Paid Thomas Season for leede to serve the churche   vj s. iiij d.

Paid for frankensence .   .   .   .   .   iij d.

Spend at the makynge of the pascalle .   .   .   .   iiij d.

Paid for rynginge of day belle at Easter to Rusberi   .   xij d.

Paid Rychard Crosse for makynge of takelynges and
nayles for the great belle   .   .   .   .   v s.

Paid Thomas Season for glassinge of the stepulle windous   xj s.

Paid for glasse for the same windous   .   .   .   vij s.

Paid towardes the hanginge of the great belle   .   .   iiij s.

Paid to John Daulton for mendynge of the antyfener
booke [3]   .   .   .   .   vj d.

Paid to Steven Knyght for nayles for the belles, for
makynge and mendinge of lockes, and a stabulle [4] to
the yate in the churche yeard   .   .   .   .   ij s. iiij d.

Paid to the pavier for his yeares wages   .   .   .   ij s. viij d.

Paid James Willes for canduls   .   .   .   .   ij d.

Paid to Johan Troyte for d. a li. of syses and canduls
to burne in the launtrne   .   .   .   .   .   xiiij d.

Paid William Powis for a belle rope for the fyrst belle .   ij s. iiij d.

Paid him more for d. a li. syses   .   .   .   vj d.

Paid for settinge the clothe over the wrode [5]   .   .   iiij d.

Paid for vij. loodes of lyme to whitlyme the churche   .   ij s. xj d.

Paid for the payver quartere wages   .   .   .   xvj d.

Paid for j. li. canduls d. Rusbery   .   .   .   iiij d.

Paid for pargyttinge the churche to Thomas Dyke   .   v s. iij d.

Paid for glassinge of saynt Margretes chaunchelle   xij d.

Paid for settinge up of the cepulcre   .   .   .   .   viij d.

---

[1] The rood.

[2] Of course, this means Dinham. It is curious that the very early form of the name
should have been preserved to so late a date.

[3] i. e. The Antiphonary.   [4] A staple.   [5] The rood.

Paid for a vesselle and a lad payle [1] to putt in lyme   .   xviij d.

Paid for charke colle   .   .   .   .   .   ij d.

Paid for makynge a stoke for on of the grett belles   .   xx d.

Paid to William Marten and John Blunt for makynge
the seid stoke   .   .   .   . vj s. viij d.

Paid to Rusbery for wyer   .   .   .   .   .   iiij d.

Paid for glassinge to Thomas Season   .   .   x s.

Paid for canduls to rynge curfur to Rusbery   •   ij d.

Paid for canduls to rynge day belle to James Willes   .   ij d.

Paid John Raulins for makynge of new baudrickes and
mendynge of the olde baudrickes .   .   .   .   xx d.

Paid to Thomas Season for glasse   .   .   .   .   xxiij d.

Paid to him for trussinge up of the great belle   .   .   iiij d.

Paid for mendynge a candellsticke for the hie auter to
Season   .   .   .   .   x d.

Paid to hym for shuttinge of a belle rope   .   .   .   ij d.

Summa totalis   .   vj li. xviij s. v d.

Recevid by me, Richard Blasfilde and Willyam Bradshalle, as here after folowythe.

Receyved at Easter of the churche money .   .   xxxj s. viij d.

Received for ser Thomas Chermes pitt   .   •   . vj s. viij d.

Received for Thomas Heytons pytt   .   .   .   . vj s. viij d.

Received for Lewes Crouther pytt   .   .   . vj s. viij d.

Received for John Taylers pytt   .   .   . vj s. viij d.

Received for T. Phelipes pytt   .   .   .   . vj s. viij d.

Received for Joane Blasfildes pytt   .   .   .   . vj s. viij d.

Received of mr Passy and An Tayler for one pue
under the pilpett, late mr Taylers   .   .   .   v s.

Received of William Justes for d. a pue at west end
the churche on the south side   .   .   .   .   xvj d.

[1] A pail for lading, still called in Northamptonshire a *lade-pail*.

Received of George Heywode for fouerth parte of a pue,
wiche was m^r Walkers, in the west ende on the
south side . . . . . . xvj d.

Received of the parisners at sondrye tymes, as here after foloyethe.

Received the xx. day of Marche	. . .	xiiij s. v d.
Received the xxvij. day of Marche	. .	vj s. v d.
Received the iij. day of July	.	vj s. iij d.
Received the x. day of July	. .	vj d.
Received the xxij. of October	. .	xv s vj d.
Received the xxx. of October	. . .	iiij s.

Summa rec.   vj li. ix s. iiij d.

Received more of John Sherman for the rent of his brique
closse, due at Mychelmas last . . xvij s. v d.

Summa rec. . . vj li. xvij s. v d.

So the churche restithe in det to them   xij s.

ffinis.

Charges leyde out be Edwarde Bagger and William Pynner, churche wardens of Ludlow in anno Domini 1559.

Payd James Willes for bawdrickes to rynge day belles, from the xvij day of November tylle Candlemas   iiij d.

Payd, the xix day of November, for a quarter of a li. of frankensence . . . .   ij d.

Payd, the xxj. of November, for a li. of candles to synge the first masse . . . . . · .   iij d. ob.

Payd, the xxvij. day, for a corde to the organs . .   j d.

Payd, the iij. day of December, for vj. yeardes iij. quarter pydelasse [1] to mende ij. of the best ropes .   vj d.

Payd for ij. yeardes and di. peny brode silke and in thryde [2] to mende the same . . .   iij d. ob.

Payd Rushebery for the mendynge of them . .   vj d.

Payd the same tyme for a li. of candles to synge the fyrst masse . . . .   iij d. ob.

Payd, the vij day of December, for half a li. of sysse .   v d. ob.

Payd for half a li. of vyssetynge candles fate by Rushebery the xx. day of November . . .   v d. ob.

Payd, the xv. day of December, for a li. of candles to rynge curfur . . . . .   iij d. ob.

Payd, the xix. day, for a li. of candles to synge the fyrst masse . . . . . .   iij d. ob.

Payd, the xxj. day, to the pavyor for his quarters wages from Mychalmas to Christmas . . .   xvj d.

Payd for yevy levys [3] to dresse the churche against Christmas . . . . .   ij d.

---

[1] I have not met with this word elsewhere.   [2] Thread.   [3] Ivy leaves.

Payd for ij li. of candles to hange in the churche on
Christmas day in the mornynge . . . .   vij d.

Payd for a li. of sysse against Christmas . . .   xj d.

Payd for a lynke the same tyme, weynge ij li. iij. quarters and di. quarter . . . . . .   x d.

Payd for half a li. of sysse · . . . .   v d. ob.

Payd for a howpe of colles [1] to sens withe . . .   j d.

Payd for mendynge of the whyle of the first belle .   j d. ob.

Payd for half a li. of sysse . . . .   v d. ob.

Payd for lycor [2] to lycor the chymes . . . .   j d.

Payd for a rope to pysse [3] the lyttelle belle rope . .   ob.

Payd, the xxx. day, for a li. of candles to rynge curfur .   iij d. ob.

Payd, the last day of December, for mendynge of the
bawdryke of the secound tenor . . . .   xij d.

Payd the same tyme for a quarter of li. of frankensens   ij d.

Payd, the iij day of January, for mendynge of the bawdryke of our Lady belle . . . . .   viij d.

Payd, the vj day of January, for half a li. of sysse .   v d. ob.

Payd William Powis, the fyrst day of February, for
ij li. iij. quarters a oz. of tryssille candelle [4] .   ij s. viij d.

Payd, the ij. day of February, for vij. fote of glasse and
ij. fote and a di. of olde glasse for the mydlemost
pane in the steple . . . . . .   v s. ij d.

Payd, the iiij day of February, to Thomas Seasson for
fastnynge of the glasse wyndowes in the churche .   ix d.

Payd, the x day of February, for a li. of candles to rynge
curfur . . . .   iij d. ob.

Payd Thomas Season for hanginge the pawle [5] over the
roode . . . .   iiij d.

Payd him for the takynge doune of ytt . . .   ij d.

---

[1] A *whope of charcoles* occurs on a former occasion. See p. 68.
[2] In the dialect of Gloucestershire, they still say *to liquor*, for to oil.
[3] To piece.   [4] This sort of candle has not been mentioned before.
[5] The pall.

Payd, the xvij day of February, for a lode of stone in the churche house . . . . . . ij s. ij d.

Payd for the caryage of ytt . . . . . vj d.

Payd, the xxj. day of February, for half a li. of vyssetynge candles . . . . . . v d. ob.

Payd Thomas Season for the keypinge of the chymes ij s. vj d.

Payd for late neayle [1] and houle nayle to the churche house . . . . j d.

Payd the pavyer for his quarters wages ended at our Lady day . . . . xvj d.

Payd Dyke the tyler for iiij. dayes worke apon the churche house . . . . ij s. viij d.

Payd, the xvj. day of Marche, for a rope to the fyrst belle . . . . ij s.

Payd for nayles to sett up the sepulcre . . . iij d.

Payd for pynes to pyne clotes [2] about ytt . . . j d.

Payd Thomas Season in fulle recompense of the ymage of the resurrexcon . . . . . . xviij d.

Payd, upon Easter even, for a bushelle of colles . . iiij d.

Payd the same tyme for half a li. of frankensence . iiij d.

Payd Thomas Season for hangynge up of the sacrynge belle in the hie chauncelle, and for a claspe of iron set apon the frame of the sepulcur . . . ij d.

Payd to the pavyor for beinge at the makynge of the pascalle . . . . iiij d.

Payd Thomas Season for makynge of the sepulcur and for takynge ytt downe . . . . . . xx d.

Payd upon Easter day in the mornynge for a sysse candle . . . . j d.

Payd Rushbery for a breakefast to the ryngers apon Blacke Monday [3] . . . . . . xij d.

[1] Lath nails; I have not met with *houle* nails before.　　[2] To pin clouts, or cloths.

[3] Black Monday was a popular name given to Easter Monday, in memory, it is said, of the severity of the weather on that day (April 14, 1360), when King Edward the Third's army, then before Paris, suffered greatly from it.

Spent at the makynge of the pascalle   .   .   .   iiij d.

Payd to William Powis for makynge of the pascalle
and a tapor over the sepulcre weyinge xiij li. and
a half .   .   .   .   xij s. iiij d.

Payd hym the same tyme for a lynke weynge ij li. and
di. and di. quarter .   .   .   .   .   viij d.

Payd, the x day of Aprelle, for a rope to our Lady belle   ij s.

Payd for nayles to mende the beyre and for the mendynge of ytt .   .   .   .   .   .   iij d.

Payd Richard Crosse for a key to the vestry dore   .   ij s.

Payd him the same tyme for a caye¹ to the steple dore
and the mendynge of the locke .   .   .   .   iij d.

Payd him more for a key to the dore of the decons
chamber .   .   .   .   iij d.

Payd him for a key to the churche howse .   .   .   ij d.

Payd for xxvij li. of sowder to mende the ledes of the
churche .   .   .   .   xiij s. vj d.

Payd William Sonkey for half a c. and vj li. of lede .   iiij s. vj d.

Payd for ij. bushelle of colles .   .   .   .   .   vj d.

Payd for a li. of tallow .   .   .   .   .   iij d.

Payd for half a li. of rossen .   .   .   .   .   j d.

Payd Thomas Jukes, tynker, for iij. dayes worke   .   ij s. ij d.

Payd William Tyler for ij. dayes worke and di.   .   xviij d.

Payd, upon Corpus Christi day, for pynes and poyntes to
dresse the canapie .   .   .   .   .   .   j d.

Payd for a brekefast to them that dyd cary the canapie   vij d.

Payd, the first day of June, for a rope to the secounde
tenor .   .   .   .   ij s.

Payd, the v. day of June, for settinge up a while to the
secounde tenor and for nayles .   .   .   .   ij d. ob.

Payd, the xviij. day of June, for mendynge of the
bawdryke of the first belle .   .   .   .   .   viij d.

¹ Key.

Payd, the xx day of June, for ij. peces of tymber to sett
    by the comunyon table and for nayles to the
    carpenter . . . . x d.
Payd, the xxiij. day of June, for takynge downe the
    table in Saynte Johns chauncelle . . . iiij d.
Payd for pynes and tackes to pyne the cloth on the
    communyon table . . . . . . j d.
Payd for whit paper for m^r Cowpers and to John Brocke
    to pryke [1] . . . . ij d.
Paid to John Dawton, the first day of July, for a bocke
    of the communyon and iij. Sawters . . . x s.
Payd George Heywode, the xxx day, for a bocke
    of the communyon and vj. Sawters, and the cariage
    of them from London . . . . . xvij s. vj d.
Payd Thomas Jukes, tynker, and his brother, for j. dayes
    worke apon the leedes . . . . . xvj d.
Payd for iij li. iij quarters of soder bestowede upon the
    leedes . . . . xxij d. ob.
Payd Richarde Swanson for vj li. and di. leede . . vj d. ob.
Payd, the xxij. day of August, for mendynge the dore
    in the churche yearde . . . . . . vij d.
Payd Steven Knyght for a hynge and mendynge of the
    other hynge . . . . viij d.
Payd, the ij. day of September, for mendynge of the beare   ij d.
Payd Steven Knyght for kepinge of the chymes from
    the v. day of October tylle the last day of October iij s. iiij d.
Payd Richarde Crosse the x day of September for mend-
    ynge a locke to the churche dore . . . ij d.
Payd, the xv. day of September, for paper to pricke
    withe . . . . ij d.
Payd the xxvj. day of September for takynge downe
    the rowde [2] . . . . vj d.

[1] *i.e.* for writing musical notes.
[2] Rood. The Protestant feelings of Elizabeth's reign are now beginning to show themselves.

Payd the pavier for his half yeres wages endede at My-
chalmas . . . .   ij s. viij d.
Payd, the xvij day of October, for my charges goinge
to Herforde satt [1] be a sitacion, beinge on the
churche behalf . . . .   ij s. vj d.
Payd James Wylles for candels to ringe day belle .   j d.
Payd, the xxv. day of October, for a li. of candles to
ringe curfur . . . .   iij d. ob.
Payd for makinge the pore mand boxe [2] . . .   xij d.
Payd for hynges and a locke . . . .   xij d.
Payd for ij. claspes of yron . . . .   xij d.
Payd for woode to melt leede to fasten the claspes of yron
in the walle . . . .   j d.
Payd Walter Bolde for iiij dayes worke takynge downe
of the auters [3] . . . .   iij s. iiij d.
Payd Thomas Season for helpinge of hym . . .   viij d.
Paid the pavier for his paynes . . . .   iiij d.
Payd for ij. bushelles of lyme to plaster the walles where
the autors was . . . .   vj d.
Payd William Stocketon for wryttinge over the poore
mans boxe . . . .   iiij d.
Payd Steven Knyght for brassynge [4] of the grett belle   viij d.
Payd John Sadler for mendynge of a bawderyke .   ij d.
Payd be my felow for makynge clene of the churche .   xvj d.
        Summa receittes . . vj li. xv s. iij d. ob.

Recevid by the churche wardens ffor the use of the churche.

Receyved for the burialle of m^r John Howcke and his
wife of the leden porche . . . . .   xiij s. iiij d.

[1] I cannot explain this word, which is clearly the reading of the manuscript.
[2] Begging-box, or alms-box.
[3] Altars.
[4] Brazing. We have before had payments for *brassynge* a candlestick.

Receyved for the burialle of m^r Dedicotte . . . vj s. viij d.

Receyved for the burialle of m^r Draper . . . vj s. viij d.

Receyved for the burialle of mr. Steyner . . vj s. viij d.

Receyved for the burialle of mother Dowbulles . . vj s. viij d.

Receyved apon Easter day in the Easter boxe . xxxj s. ix d.

Receyved of the parisheners towarde the reparacon of
the churche . . . . liij s. v d.

Receyved of William Owen for a pew in the sowthe
yelle,[1] that was Rycharde Tomlyns . . . ij s. iiij d.

Summa totallis receites . . vij li. iij s. ix d. ob.

So we rest in the churche dett . vij s. ij d.

Grauntede to Richard Tomlyns one littelle pew on the
south syd the churche, late Richard Waties, in
consideracon of the forseide pew by hym surrendrede to the use of William Owen.

So the churche oweth them . . . . ij s. xj d.

Grauntede to Edward Bager and William Pynner, late
churche wardens, one pew nere the fonte on the
southe side, late in the occupacon of John Hoke,
and payd for a fyne over the forseid debet, xx d. delyvered to the newe churche wardens.

ffinis.

Charges layd out upon the reparacons of the parish
churche of Ludlow by Thomas Langford and John
Taylor, wardens, from the feast of Alle Seyntes anno
Domini 1559, unto the seyde feast then next ensuynge viz. for one hole yere, anno Domini 1560.

In primis, for russes to straye[2] the seate before the pilpett . . . . ij d.

Paid James Wylles for candels to rynge day belle . vj d.

---

[1] Aisle.   [2] Rushes to strew.

Paid Richard Crosse for a stapulle and a haspe for the
    poore mans chest . . . . .   iij d.
Paid for a locke for the same cheste . . . .   iiij d.
Paid for lyme to washe and plaster the walle where
    the auctor [1] stode in the hie chaunselle . .   iiij d.
Paid John Umfres for half a dayes worke there . .   iiij d.
Paid Steven Knyght for ij. ynges and a stapulle for the
    churche yerde yate . . . . .   xij d.
Paid for settinge the lege upon the same yeatt . .   ij d. ob.
Paid John the kerver for translatynge the tabulle .   ij s. ij d.
Paid for nayles for the same . . . .   j d.
Paid William Powis for a li. of syses . . .   **x** d.
Paid Styven Knyght and Rushbery for the kepinge of
    the chymes alle the yere . . . . . vj s. viij d.
Paid for wier to amende the chymes at sundry tymes .   xij d.
Paid Richarde Lawfyld for the carege of xx lode of
    dounge from the grate . . . . .   xvj d.
Paid John Umfries for iiij. dayes worke, ij. dayes upon
    the grate, and ij. dayes in mendynge of the walle
    by the almehousse . . . . . . ij s. viij d.
Paid Collyns iij. dayes worke upon the same . .   xxj d.
Paid Richard Lowfylde for the careg of ij. lode of saunde
    for the same walle . . . . .   ij d.
Paid for vj. busshelles of lyme to amend the same walle
    at . . . .   xviij d.
Paid the kerver for settynge in a post and a ralle [2] over
    the grate, and nayles for the same . . .   vj d.
Paid Thomas Season for mendynge of a kandelstyke .   xij d.
Do. John Broke a quyer of paper . . . .   iiij d.
Paid Umfry pavyer for ivye to hange in the body of the
    churche . . . .   iiij d.
Paid for ij. li. of kandelles to hange in the body of the
    churche . . . .   vij d.

[1] The altar.   [2] A rail.

Paid William Marten for ij dayes worke and a half upon
the great belstoke and whyle . . . ij s. iij d.
Paid for naylez for the same . . . . iij d.
Paid John Wryght for the mendynge of the bere, and
for nayles . . . . iij d.
Paid for a fote for the bere. . . . . iiij d.
Paid Raufe Harvy and Thomas Season for vij fote and
d. of glasse sett up in saynt Margrettes chaun-
selle in the northe window . . . . v s.
Paid them more for settinge up of iij fotte of olde glasse
in the same window . . . . . . xij d.
More paid them for vj fote of new glasse sett up in our
Lady chauncelle in the next window to the dore
upon the southe side . . . . . iiij s. iiij d.
More paid them for settinge up of iiij fote of olde glasse
in the window above in the same chaunselle . xvj d.
More paid Thomas Marten for a fotte for the bere . iiij d.
Paid Umfry pavier for his hole yeres wages . . v s. iiij d.
Paid for the makynge of our boke at the vysitacion . x d.
Paid Rusheberie for a brekefast for the ryngers . . xij d.
Paid for the makynge clene of the stepulle steyrez . iiij d.
Paid Thomas Season for mendynge and fasteninge the
window over the wedinge churche dore[1] . . vj s. viij d.

---

[1] The wedding door has been frequently mentioned in these accounts. Before the Reformation, important parts of the Services of baptism, matrimony, and the churching of
women, were performed at the church door, usually in the porch. The reader of Chaucer
will remember what he says (*Cant. T. l.* 462) of the Wife of Bath,—
    " Housbondes *atte chirche dore* hadde sche fyfe."
It is for this reason, no doubt, that we find holy-water stoups so commonly in old porches
of churches. It was directed in the will of Henry VI. that there should be " in the south
side of the body of the church of Eton College a fair large dore with a porche, and the
same for christeninges of children and weddinges." At the southern entrance of Norwich
Cathedral, there is a representation of the Sacrament of marriage carved in stone. The
custom was that the parties did not enter the church till that part of the office when the
minister now goes up to the altar and repeats the Psalm. Part of the ceremony under the
porch consisted also in the endowing of the bride, which was called *dos ad ostium eccle-*

Paid Hervye for viij. fotte of glasse sett up in the stepulle
    in the west window .   .   .   .   .   v s. iiij d.
Paid Stevyn Knyght for mendynge of the cloke   .   viij d.
Delivered Rushberie at sundry tymes to rynge curfur
    vj. pound of candles .   .   .   .   xxj d.
Paid Humfry pavyer for makinge clene the windowes in
    the body of the churche .   .   .   .   iiij d.
Paid Rushberie for makinge clene of the leedes . . ij d.
Paid Thomas a Crew for mendynge of a bawderyke . ij d.
Paid Richarde Crosse for mendynge of the keye and
    locke of the wed [1] northe churche dore. . . ij d.
Paid John Clee for mendynge the key and loke of the
    stepulle dore .   .   .   .   .   .   ij d.
Paid Richard Shamsey for ij belle ropes . iij s. iiij d.
More paid hym for on belle rope .   .   . ij s. iiij d.
Paid William Powis for d. li. of syses . . v d.
Paid Thomas Season for j li. and half of sowder that he
    dyde bestow upon the northe yelle [2] . . . ix d.
Paid Thomas Season for settynge up of iiij fotte of
    glasse in saynt Katherne chaunselle in the southe
    window .   .   .   .   xij d.
Paid hym for ij. fotte of payntede glasse for the same
    plasse .   .   .   .   xij d.
Paid Thomas Season and others for pollynge downe the
    seate where our Ladie stode in our Lady chaunselle xx d.
Paid Walter Bolde for makynge up of the same walle
    agayne .   .   .   .   xxij d.
Paid for lyme to make up the walle .   .   . ij s. iiij d.
Paid William Marten for on dayes worke and a half for
    hym and ij men, upon the belstokes and whyles of
    the seconde tenor and our Lady belle . . iij s. v d.

sic. The door at which the wedding was performed appears to have been generally on
the southern side of the church, but at Ludlow it was evidently not the porch, and, from
an entry a few lines further on, it would appear to have been on the north side.
    [1] So in the MS., but no doubt a mere error of the scribe for _reedinge_.   [2] Aisle.

Paid Thomas Season for settynge up xlj foote of glasse
in the stepulle, that is to saye, viij fotte and d. in
the north window, xvj fotte in the west window,
viij fotte and half in the south window, and the
rest beinge vij fotte in mendynge of other paynes
there as shall appere at x. . . . . . xxx s.

More paid hym for settinge up of xxij foote of olde
glasse in the stepulle, beynge in v paynes, that is
to saye, on in the west window, and iij in the southe
window . . . . vj s. v d.

Paid Steven Knyght for xvij li. of iron beinge made in
smalle barres for the staye of the paynes of glasse
in the stepulle . . . . iiij s. iij d.

Paid for a planke to knele upon at the communyon
tabulle . . . . iiij d.

Paid James Wylles for j li. of candles . . iij d. ob.

Summa totalis of the charges vj li. xj d.

Receites for this yere.

Received of the paris at Easter . . . . xxviij s.

Received of the parysnors, as be quartors contributors
unto the reparacion of the churche . . . l s. vj d. ob.

Received for the burialle of a chylde of Thomas Raynolde
chylde . . . . vj s. viij d.

Received for the burialle of m^r Masones mother . vj s, viij d.

Received for the burialle of m^r Hoke . vj s. viij d.

Received for the burialle of William Beke . vj s. viij d.

Received for the burialle of m^r Walker . . vj s. viij d.

Received for the burialle of m^r Bekes wif . . vj s. viij d.

Received for a pew sett unto William Pewes and Robert Wryght, beinge in the northe yelle beneth the
churche dore . . . . iiij s. viij d.

Received for a pew sett unto Heughe Gryffetes and
Hughe ap Powelle in the same yelle . . . ij s. viij d.

Received for half a pew sett unto John Raulens in the
   body of the churche, benethe the ffounte on the
   northe syde, withe Thomas Ward .   .   .   ij s.

Received for a pew sett unto John Mathese, surrendrede
   by Edmounde Bowlande for hym, wiche standethe
   in the southe yelle .   .   .   .   .   .   xij d.

Received for half a pew sett unto John Huke, wiche was
   his fathers, wiche lyeth the next pew to the longe
   seate before the pilpytt in the body of the churche   ij s. iiij d.

Received of William Powes for the stoune wiche was
   taken doune in our Lady chaunselle .   .   .   iiij s.

      Summa totalis recevide .   .   vj li. xv s. ij. d. ob.
      So rest dew to the parishe .   xiij s. ix d. ob.

Received for the holy loffe from xix. of November after
   v d. ob. wyke, 1559, untylle the 3. of November
   wiche commethe to .   .   .   .   . xxiiij s. iij d. ob.

Paid herof unto Elnor Baylie, for the kepynge of a
   chylde, ij d. a wyke, from the xxiij. of December
   untille the xxx. of November .   .   .   . viij s. ij d.

Paid John Cleys wife ij d. a wyke from the 12. of January 1559 untylle the 17. of August 1560, and after
   every weeke a j d. untylle the 4. of October .   v s. xj d.

Paid Johane of Galvarde¹ ij d. a wyke from the 25. of
   Januarye untylle the 3. of August .   . iiij s. viij d.

Paid Bellyngames wiffe ij d. a wyke from the xth of
   August untylle the 30. of November .   . ij s. x d.

      Sum payde .   xxj s. vij d.
      So rest .   . ij s. viij d. ob.

Sum totallis of receites as apperith by booke vij li. xix s. vj d. ob.
      Sum of paymentes .   . vij li. ij s. vj d.
So the churche wardens rest in dett withe xx d.
      of the last churche wardens recevyd xviij s. viij d.

¹ For Goalford, no doubt.

Wiche is paide and quyte and delyvered to the churche wardens of new electede.

finis.

The accomptes of Simon Thornton and John Brasier, churche wardens of the towne of Ludlow, from the feast of Simon and Jude in the yeare of our Lord 1560, unto the saide feast in the yeare 1561.

November.

In primis, the 30. day, for packe threde to mende the clocke . . . . ob.

December.

Item, the 1 day, to James Willes for candles to ringe the day belle unto Candlmas . . . . . vj d.

Item, the iiij. day, a li. of sises to serve the quere . x d.

Item, the viij. day, delivered to Rushbury, a pounde of candles to rynge curfur . . . . . iiij d.

Item, the same day, for iij. barres of iron to William Idwyn to sett in the glasse windowes in the steple xviij d.

Item, the 9. day, a belle rope for the yelde [1] belle ij s. vij d. ob.

Item, the 12. day, to Thomas Seasson for settinge up 15 iron barres in the glasse windowes in the steple, and mendynge 30 quarelles [2] in west ende of the same, and mendinge the grate at the churche style and the gate at the college. . . . . iij s.

Item, for lyme to dresse the same windowes at the same tyme . . . . ob. q^{a}.

Item, the 22. day, for a corde to hange the lantern, and for a keie to the poore mens boxe, to Richarde Carver . . . . vij d. ob.

Item, a li. of candles to hange in the body of the church upon Christmas day . . . . . . iij d. ob.

---

[1] Guild. [2] Panes of glass.

Item, to the paviers maide, for makinge cleane the remainder of the tabernacle in our Lady chauncelle .   ob. qª.
Item, the 24. of December, to Rusheburie, a li. of candles
   to rynge curfur   .   .   .   .   .   .   iij d. ob.
Item, to the pavier for his wages for Christmas quarter   xvj d.
Item, the same tyme, for a belle and whipcorde to make
   a whipe to drive dogges out of the churche [1]   .   j d. ob.

January.

Item, the 1. day, a li. of syses   .   .   .   .   x d.
Item, the v. day, for whippinge the seconde belle rope .   ij d.
Item, the 7. day, a li. of candles to sett in the lantern to
   lyght at the morninge prayer .   .   .   .   .   iij d. ob.
Item, the 10. day, to Rushburie, a li. of candles to rynge
   curfur withe   .   .   .   .   iij d. ob.
Item, the 30. day, to Rushburie and Thomas Season to-
   warde kepinge of the chymes   .   .   .   .   ij s.
Item, the same day, for mendynge the lantern and twise
   hanginge it uppe   .   .   .   .   .   .   xx d.
Item, a li. of wyre for the chymes   .   .   .   .   viij d.

February.

Item, to Thomas Carver, for makinge a new cradle for
   the bere, and naylynge the yointes of the beere,
   and other wise mendynge the same   .   .   .   xx d.

Marche.

Item, the 1. day, d. li. of sise, to say morninge prayer,
   yeven [2] Rushburie   .   .   .   .   .   .   v d.
Item, the same tyme, geven Rushberie to paye for mak-
   inge his surples.   .   .   .   . ix d. ob. qª.

---

[1] Allusions to this custom have occurred before. See p. 15. It may be remarked that this office was not confined to England, and it appears to have been of some antiquity. It is men-
tioned in the "Contes d'Eutrapel," by the well known French satirical writer of the sixteenth century, Noel du Fail, who, in one of his facetious stories, the scene of which lay in a monastery, says, " survient un quidam enfroqué, ayant la charge d'éteindre les chandelles et chasser les chiens hors d'église." (Contes d'Eutrapel, Conte xx.) The dog-whipper here was a monk, enfroqué.   [2] Given.

Item, the iij. day, to Rushburie, to ringe curfur, a
pounde of candles . . . . . . iij d. ob.
Item, the 22. paid for mendinge the longe seate beneathe
the pulpit . . . . . . ob. qᵃ.
Item, the same tyme, paid James Willes a quarter wages
for kepinge dogges out of the churche, betwixt
Christmas and Easter . . . . . xij d.
Item, the 26. day, at the visitacion, paid for the table of
commaundementes and the new kalender . . xviij d.
Item, the 27. day, for shwipinge ¹ the walles of the
churche, one dayes wages to the pavier, and Thomas Willes . . . . xvj d.
Item, the same day, to the pavier, for one quarters
wages . . . . xvj d.
Item, the 29. day, to Crosse, for a key for the boxe to
serve at Easter . . . . iij d.

Aprelle.

Item, the 1. day, a li. and d. of glewe to mende bothe
the bellowes of the great organs . . . ix d.
Item, a corde for the bellows of the same organs, the
same day . . . . j d.
Item, the iiij. day, to Thomas Season, for settinge the table
of the commaundementes in a frame, and mendynge
the bellowes of the great organs, and clensinge the
same, withe other worke done about the same iij s.
Item, the 7. day, to Rushburie for a brekefast for ringe-
inge day belle at Easter . . . . . xij d.
Item, the 23. day, to Rushburie, to ringe curfer, in candles . . . . iij d. ob.
Item, the 25. in ernest to mende the glase windowes . iij s. iiij d.
Item. the 25. day, paid for a pulley for third bellow
that had not ben occupiede of longe . . . ij d.

¹ Sweeping.

Item, the said 25. more for keypinge the chymes, paide
    to Thomas Season   .   .   .   .   .   .   ij s.
Item, the 28. to the pavier, for a stone to ley before the
    quyre dore   .   .   .   .   .   .   j d. ob.

Maii.

Item, the 3. day, to Edward the carier, for a Bible, and
    the cariage of the same from London, and my lettres
    to London   .   .   .   .   xij s. v d.
Item, the same tyme, paid by the commandementes of
    m^r baylives, for dressinge ther seate for my lord
    president [1]   .   .   .   .   vj d.
Item, the 20. day, the rest of the money for reparinge alle
    the windowes in the churche withe glasse   .   xxiij s. iiij d.

June.

Item, the xx. day, for a belle rope for the seconde tenor   xxij d.
Item, the 23. day, for a rope for the great pvise [2] of the
    clocke   .   .   .   .   xxij d.
Item, paid for makinge cleane the staires of the steple,
    the 24. day   .   .   .   .   iij d.
Item, the same tyme, for makinge a grate at the college
    dore   .   .   .   .   ij s. iijd.
Item, paid for karienge away the yearthe where the
    grate was made   .   .   .   .   .   .   iiij d.
Item, the 27. day, paid for a giste [3] to mende the leste [4]
    of the belle fery [5]   .   .   .   .   .   .   xij d.
Item, paid for carienge away the dust that came out of
    the belle soller [6]   .   .   .   .   vj d.

[1] This was no doubt Sir Henry Sydney, newly appointed to the high office of Lord President of Wales and the Marches.

[2] Apparently for parvis. The parvis was the open place before the porch or entrance to a church, and it may here mean the place before the clock.

[3] A joist?   [4] I do not know this word.

[5] The belfry   [6] The sollar, or upper room.

Item, the same tyme, paid for ij ropes to hange the
lesser peise [1] of the clocke . . . . . ij s.
Item, the same tyme, for ij fealde and a lader that serv-
eth in the steple or soller . . . . . xx d.
Item, paid John Blunt, his prentice, and a laborer,
workeinge about the yelde belle and the steple . v s. x d.

July.

August.

Item, paid Crosse, the x. day, for a quarter and iiij li. of
iron, and workeinge the same, withe the rest of iron
worke mendinge, belonginge to the yelde belle . vij s.
Item, the 13. day, for mendynge the locke of the steple
dore . . . . j d.

September.

Item, the 15. day, a quyre of paper to Trueman . . iiij d.
Item, the 22. day, a li. of candles to the decon to rynge
curfer . . . . iij d.
Item, the 25. for mendinge the bawdrickes of iij belles xx d.
Item, the same tyme, for lyme and to the workemen one
the leades . . . . vij s. viij d.
Item, at the chauncelors visitacion, for iij bookes . iiij d.
Item, the same tyme, for the copie of the presentment vj d.

October.

Item, the ij. for soder, to mend the leades . . . ij s. ix d.
Item, to Thomas Season sonne, for helpinge his father
upon the leades . . . . . . iiij d.
Item, for woode to worke the same soder by . . ij d.
Item, the iij. day, sises to say the mornynge prayer by ij d.

[1] Weight.

Item, the 19. day, sises to serve the quyre d. li. .   v d.
Item, the same day, a li. of candles to the deacon   .   iij d.
Item, the 20. paide Trueman for prickinge sertayne
        bookes . . . .   v s.
Item, the same tyme, to Thomas Langforde, a surples for
        the deacon . . . .   v s.
Item, makinge the same surples   .   .   .   .   viij d.
Item, paid for pesinge a belle rope, to Thomas Season   ij d.
Item, the same tyme, paid to the pavier for half yeres
        wages . . . .   ij s. viij d.
Item, about that tyme, to the paviers wif, ij burden of
        rushes, and makinge cleane mr baylives seat   .   iiij d.
Item, the 31. day. d. li. of syses to the deacon   .   v d.
Item, to the decon, for shotinge a belle rope   .   .   ij d.
Item, to the person, for a booke of the Homyles   .   xiiij d.
Item, to ser Richarde Cooper for kepinge the regester of
        christninges, weddinges, and burialles   .   .   ij s.
Item, to Elnor Baylie, for the poore childe sins myne
        accompt of the poore mens money geven upe   .   ij d.
Item, the last of October, a li. of candles to rynge cur-
        fer . . . .   iij d.
Item, the same day, half a li. of syses to the decon for
        the morninge prayer . . . . . .   v d.
            Sum totallis   .   vj li. xj s. ob.

Receptes.

In primis, receavide at our entrye of mr baylives   .   xij s.
Item, for the quarterige . . . . . . iij li. ij s.
Item, at Easter . . . . . . xlvj s. viij d.
Item, one burialle in the churche for mrs Burge Jevans vj s. viij d.
Item, one pewe, wiche was late mrs Jevance, beinge
        behinde the churche doore, sett to William Clun-
        tone . . . . iiij s. viij d.

Item, one pewe, late Thomas Rushburies, under the
    clocke howse, lett to Robert Beddow and Edward
    Hintone . . . .   iiij s.
Item, one pewe, late Howelle Glovers, above the pil-
    pett, lett to William Powis   .   .   .   iiij s.
           Sum of the receptes   .   .   vij li.
      So the churche wardens owe to the churche   viij s. xj d. ob.
                  Wiche is paide.
Receyvede of m^r John Sharmon for the bricke closse   .   viij s.
        Sum .   .   .   xvj s. xj d. ob.
Wiche is delyverede to the other churche wardens John
    ap Guylliam and William Powis as above   xvj s. xj d. ob.
                Finis.

Charges leyde out for the reparacions of the pareshe
churche of Ludlow by John Gwylliam and William
Powis, churche wardens of the same pareshe, anno
Domini 1562.

In primis, delyvered to the deacon the vij. day of Novem-
    ber, candles j pounde   .   .   .   .   .   iij d.
Item, delyvered to the deacon that day d. a li. scyses   v d.
Item, delivered the deacon, the xvj. day of November,
    candles j li. .   .   .   .   .   .   iij d.
Item, delivered the deacon, the xxvj. day of November,
    candles j li. .   .   .   .   .   .   iij d.
Item, delivered the deacon, the vj. day of December,
    candles j li. .   .   .   .   .   .   iij d.
Item, delivered that day scyses d. li   .   .   .   v d.
Item, delivered the deacon, on the iij. Sonday of Advent,
    candles j li. .   .   .   .   .   .   iij d.
Item, delivered the deacon on Christmas yeven,[1] candles
    j li. .   .   .   .   iij d·

              [1] Even, or Eve.

Item, paid for holy and evy [1] that day .   .   .   .   iiij d.

Item, delivered the bellman on Christmas yeven, for to
hange in the body of the churche, candles on pounde   iij d.

Item, delivered the deacon that day, of seyses j li.   .   x d.

Item, delivered the deacon, on saynt Stevens day, a
rope for the secounde belle   .   .   .   .   ij s. iiij d.

Item, paid to Thomas a Crue, the last Sonday of Advent,
for a bawdricke for the thirde belle   .   .   .   xx d.

Item, for a rope for the secounde tenor, on Childermas
day   .   .   .   .   ij s. iiij d.

Item, to the deacon on newyers day, candles j. li.   .   iij d.

Item, to the deacon on Sonday after xij. day, candles j li.   iij d.

Item, to the deacon, the xx. day of January, candles j li.   iij d.

Item, to the deacon, the xxiiij. day of January, seyses
quarter li.   .   .   .   .   ij d. ob.

Item, paid to the bellman for his quarteris wages deue
at Christmas   .   .   .   .   xvj d.

Item, to the deacon on Candlmas yeven,[2] candles j li. .   iij d. ob.

Item, paid mendinge a locke for the steple dore, the iiij.
day of February   .   .   .   .   .   .   iiij d.

Item, paid for nayles that day   .   .   .   .   .   ij d.

Item, paid to Thomas Season for settynge in a barre of
the churche callens [3]   .   .   .   .   .   .   ij d.

Item, to the deacon, the xxv. of February, for syeses   .   j d.

Item, to the deacon, the xxvj. of that moneth, quarter
li. seyses   .   .   .   .   ij d. ob.

Item, to the bellman, the xij. day of Februarie, in nayles
for the bere   .   .   .   .   j d.

Item, paid for settinge in a bare in the churche skallens [3]
the xiiij. of February   .   .   .   .   .   ij d.

---

[1] Holly and ivy.   [2] Candlemas eve.

[3] *Callends*, or *callens*, or, as it is called in another place, skallends, was the name given
here and in one or two other localities, to the liche-gate, or entrance through which a corpse
was carried into the church-yard, and where it rested. The passage by which the porch
of the church of Ludlow is approached from the town still bears the name, and no doubt
occupies its site.

Item, paid to John Blunt, for workeinge aboute the belles,
the xxij. day of Marche - . . . . . iiij s. viij d.

Item, paid that tyme, to Rycharde Crosse, for makinge
steropes, [1] brases, and nayles, and for shuttynge the
claper of the seconde belle . . . . . ij s. viij d.

Item, paid to Raffe the carpenter, for hanginge and
mendinge the seconde belle, the xxvj. day of Aprelle xij d.

Item, paid to Steven Knyght, for ij peces of iron that
wer occupiede about the seyde belle that tyme . ij d.

Item, to the deacon, the ij. of May, for d. li. weyer [2]
for the chymes . . . . . . vj d.

Item, to Johan Dudson, on Whytsown yeven, for car-
ringe stones and lyme out of seynt Johns chauncelle . . . . iiij d.

Item, paid Rycharde Swaynsone that day for spyke nayles
to make the pewe in the seyde chauncelle . . vj d.

Item, paid Johan Dudson, the xxvij. of May, for makynge clene the same chauncelle . . . . ij d.

Item, paid the parctor [3] for a booke of Omelyes to be rede
in the Rogasion weke . . . . . iiij d.

Item, paid for j seme [4] of whitlyme, to pave in saynt
Johns chaunselle, the first of June . . . viij d.

Item, paid for woode to make fyer on the ledes of the
churche, the iiij. and v[th] and the viij. dayes of
August . . . . xij d.

Item, paid to Thomas Season, the iiij. day of Aprelle, for
mendinge the glasse wyndowes in our Lady chapelle, seynt Kathern and seynt Johnes chaunselle,
that were broken . . . . . . v s.

Item, paid to Richarde Swanson, for naylles that were
occupiede about the belles, the xx[th] of Marche . iij d.

---

[1] Stirrups, perhaps here, steps for mounting. - ⸿ ⸿ ⸿ ⸿ ⸿
[2] Wire.   [3] The apparitor.
[4] A measure which has been frequently mentioned before.

Item, paid to the bellman for his quarters wages dew at
    Easter . . . .   xvj d.
Item, paid the bellman, the last of June, for his quarters
    wages due at Mydsomer . . . . .   xvj d.
Item, for thele to mende the churche dore, and a klyfft [1]
    to make steyes for the belle whelles, the xxij. of
    Marche . . . .   vj d.
Item, paid Thomas Season, for vij li. of sowder the last
    day of July . . . .   iij s. vj d.
Item, paid James Wylles that day, for ij dayes worke
    upon the ledes . . . . . .   viij d.
Item, paid to Thomas Season, the viij. day of August,
    for iiij. pounde of sowder . . . . .   ij s.
Item, paid to James Willes that day for workinge one the
    ledes . . . .   iiij d.
Item, paid to ser Richard Coper, for keypinge the booke
    of buryalles and christenynges, the fyrst day of
    August . . . .   ij s.
Item, delivered to the deacon, the xix. day of August, a
    rope for the secounde belle . . . . .   ij s. viij d.
Item, to the bellman, the xx. day of September, for a
    corde for the bellowes of the organs . . .   j d.
Item, to the deacon, on seynt Myghelles day, j li. candles   iij d.
Item, to the deacon, the iiij. day of October, d. li.
    seyses . . . .   v d.
Item, paid to Richarde Swaynson, for a rope for the iij.
    belle, the iiij. day of October . . . .   ij s. ij d.
Item, paid to the same Richarde for nayles that were
    had at dyvers tymes . . . . . .   ix d.
Item, to the deacon, the vj. day of October, j li. candles   iij d.
Item, to the deacon, the xvj. day of October, j li. candles iij d.
Item, paid the bellman, the xix. day of October, for
    his quarters wages dew at Myghellmas . .   xvj d.

_____
[1] I have not met with this word, or thele, before.

Item, paid the xx. day of October, for iij large bellropes   xiiij s.

Item, paid to m^r Alsope, for makynge our booke to gether our quarterege by   .   .   .   .   viij d.

Item, paid to Thomas a Crue, for mendinge the bawdrickes of ij belles   .   .   .   .   iiij d.

Item, paid for a pece of tymber, to make ij barres in the churche skallans, the sawinge and settinge in, and for naylles for the same   .   .   .   vj d.

Item, to the deacon, the xxiiij. day of October, j li. candles   .   .   .   .   iij d.

Item, paid for a rope for the pece of the clocke, the xxvij. day of October   .   .   .   .   viij s.

Item, paid to William Hardinge, for helpinge the deacon to mende the chymes, the xxvj. of October   .   iiij d.

Item, to the deacon, the last day of October, j li. candles   iij d.

Item, for j li. of seyses, to the deacon that day   .   .   x d.

Item, paid to Elnor Baylie that day towarde the kepinge of a chylde   .   .   .   .   .   iiij d.

Item, paid to ser Richarde Coper, for his paynes taken the feast of Easter   .   .   .   .   xij d.

Item, paid to Elnor Baylie, towardes the keypinge of a chylde   .   .   .   .   .   iiij d.

Item, paid to Thomas Season, for mendinge and makinge fast the glasse in the steple   .   .   xvj d.

Item, paid to Thomas Season, for mendinge the glasse windowes in our Lady chanselle, seynt Katerens chanselle, and in the steple   .   .   .   .   vj s. viij d.

Item, paid to the deacon, the vij. day of November, for reparacions of the chymes for this yere endide at Alle Sayntes last   .   .   .   .   vj s. viij d.

Item, paid the deacon that day, for pesynge of belleropes   viij d.

      Sum tottallis   .   .   iiij li. xij s. ix d.

Item, bestowede by m^r Farre, as hyt apere by his bylle of acompt   .   .   .   .   .   .   xlj s. j d.

So that ther is bestowede in the hoole this yere upon the
    reparacions of the churche the som of   .   vj li. xiij s. xd.

Item, for j li. candles, the vij. of November   . .   iij d.

Item, paid to the bellman for carienge of sande into
    seynt Johns chanselle   . .   .   .   .   iiij d.

        Sum tottallis of alle reparacons vj li. xiiij s. iij d. ob.

Money receyvede to the youse[1] of the churche, by John Gwilliam and William Powis, churche wardens, anno Domini 1562.

Receyvede of Annes Maylarde, xxiiij. day of November,
    1562, of the cherytie money   .   .   .   .   xvj d.

Received of Robert Hoper, the xvj. day of Merche, for
    his wifes burialle   .   .   .   .   .   .   vj s. viij d.

Received of m[r] Blassefilde, the xxv. day of May, for his
    wiffes burialle   .   .   .   .   .   .   vj s. viij d.

Received of James David ap Hoelle, the xxv. daye of
    June, for his doughters burialle   .   .   vj s. viij d.

Received of m[rs] Caper, the xxvj. day of October, for her
    husbandes burialle   ·   .   ·   ·   ·   vj s. viij d.

Received of Richarde Heyton that day, for his wifes
    burialle   .   .   .   .   vj s. viij d.

Item, we dyd sett to Richarde Heyton half a pewe in the
    northe yle of the churche that day, that was some
    tyme in the holdinge of Water Symcox   .   .   ij s. vj d.

Received of m[r] bayly Farre,[2] withe his bylle of account   iij s. ij d.

Item, that we sett a pew in the midle yle of the
    churche, that was lat in the holdynge of m[r] William
    Phellypes, to John Guilliam and Charles Boothe,
    for the some of   .   .   .   .   v s.

---

[1] The use.

[2] According to the list of bailiffs printed in my History of Ludlow, p. 493, William Poughnill and Richard Starr were elected bailiffs in 1561. The latter name is no doubt an error of the copyist for Farr.

Item, that we set Robert Gardener a pece of grounde,
    under the stayre of the clocke house, for to bylde
    hym a pewe upon, for the some of   .   .   .   ij s.
Item, we received in the churche, at the feast of Easter,
    of people that dyde receve the communyon   .   xliij s.
Received of Annes Lewys, of the cherytie money   .   vj d.
Received of the quarterege in the churche towardes the
    reparacion of the same churche   .   .   . iij li. iiij s. vij d.
Item, alowede mr Farre his reseyt of   .   .   .   . xlj s. j d.
Received of mr Partryge, for his wifes burialle, the viij.
    of this monethe   .   .   .   .   .   .   vj s. viij d.
Received of mr Hollande that day, for his wifes burialle vj s. viij d.
Received of Thomas Bedow that day, for his wifes
    burialle   .   .   .   .   vj s. viij d.
       Summa tottallis of alle receittes x li. xvj s. vj d.
      Wherof paide in reparacions, as appereth by bylle
              vj li. xiiij s. iij d. ob.
  So the churche wardens owe to the churche upon this
     accounte   .   .   iiij li. ij s. ij d. ob.
  Wherof ther is deductede   .   .   .   ij s. ob.
Wiche some of iiij li. delyvered in stocke to Richarde Swanson
  and Richard Hokke, churche wardens of new electede.
              Finis.

Charges layde out by Richarde Swanson and Richarde Houke upon the churche of Ludlow, beinge churche wardens anno Domini 1563.

Item, paid the 3. day of November, for drynkeinge at mr
    baylie Drapers [1] house   .   .   .   .   . ij s. iiij d.
Delivered the deacon at sondry tymes xix li. of candles
    at iij d. a pounde   .   .   .   .   . iiij s. ix d.
Item, to the deacon for a lytelle booke   .   .   . ij d.

---

[1] The bailiffs this year were, according to the list quoted in a former note, Robert
Mason and John Holland. The name of Draper does not appear in the list as a bailiff.

Item, paid m^r baylie Alsope, the 15. day of November, to paye the coste of vj men to Brigenorthe	xv s.
Item, paid for j pounde of syse	x d.
Item, paid Thomas Season, the 6. day of December, for mendinge the lantorne, and corde for yt - -	xix d.
Delivered to the belman, upon Christmas yve, ij li. of candles	vj d.
Item, paid for ivy and hollye that day	iiij d.
Item, paid Steven Knyght, for ij hokes for the belle ropes	ij d.
Item, for nayles to mende the bere	ij d.
Item, paid to Richarde Crosse for makynge stapulles and springes for the chymes	viij d.
Item, paid Thomas Season, for mendinge the chymes and the barrelle and jake¹ of the clockehouse	viij d.
Item, for half a belle rope	x d.
Item, paid m^r baylie Alsop, for the makinge of the booke of the parisners names	viij d.
Item, one Christmas yve, j li. of syses	x d.
Item, paid, the x. day of Aprelle, for ij bushelles of lyme	viij d.
Delivered Truman j quyre of paper	iiij d.
Item, to the pavier, a corde to the organs	ij d.
Item, paid for certeyn tymber and bordes to mende the comen pewes	iij s. viij d.
Item, paid Ivan the carpender and his man, for iij dayes worke upon the same pewes, after ix. [d. each]	iiij s. vj d.
Item, paid Thomas Dycke and Thomas Williams, for brushinge the churche walles, beinge iij dayes	v s. ij d.
Item, paid one Christofer, for seke John Lyngam	iiij d.
Item, paid to Thomas Season, for mendinge two holes in the glasse window in the wen'² chauncelle	ij d.
Item, to the belle man, j corde for the organs	ij d.
Paid for nayles to mende the churche callans	iiij d.
Paid, the xj. day of May, for a pece of tymber and ij bordes, to mende the callandes	xvj d.

¹ The jack.   ² So it is written abbreviated in the manuscript.

Item, paid Lloyde, for half a dayes worke there . . vj d.

Paid the deacon, the xij. of May, for the ringers broke-
fast . . . . xij d.

Item, paid for the weshinge of the table clothes and the
towels . . . . iiij d.

Paid to the deacon for pessinge of a belle rope . . ij d.

Item, paid Thomas a Crue, the 3. of May, for makinge
of a bawdricke . . . . xx d.

Paid John Daulton, for bringinge of a booke for the
parishe . . . . ij s.

Paid John Dalton, for an Omelye booke . . . iij s. iiij d.

Paid to hym for a lyttle booke for m^r parson . . vj d.

Paid for the copie of serteyn articles at my lordes bi-
shopes visitacon . . . . . . vj d.

Paid unto Jordeyn and Thomas Turner and ij laborers,
for the brasinge of iij belles . . . . iiij s. viij d.

Paid Richarde Crosse, for nayles and other nessarie thinges
for the same belles . . . . . ij s. x d.

Paid for a belle rope . . . . . . ij s. vj d.

Paid for a rope for the chymes and cariage of hym . iiij s. ij d.

Paid for xviij li. and a half of soder, at vj d. li., and delivered to Thomas Season . . . . ix s. iij d.

Item, in rossen . . . . . . j d.

Item, in wood and coles . . . . . . xij d.

Paid to Thomas Season man, for v dayes worke one the
leades withe hym . . . . . . iij s.

Item, paid Thomas Crue, for pessinge and mendinge iij
bawdrickes . . . . xij d.

Item, paid for j lode of lyme . . . . . vj d.

Item, paid John Salsburie, for makynge of a grest[1] for
my lorde to knele upon . . . . . iiij d.

Payd for a peyse of tymber for the same . . . vj d.

Paid the deacon, for pessinge iij belle ropes . vj d.

Item, for swepinge the steple steyres . . . iij d.

[1] This word appears to mean a cushion, or stool.

Paid for the mendinge of the bere, and nayles and
claspes of iron and tymber   .   .   .   .   xij d.
Item, delivered the deacon, the xj. day of October, j li.
and quarter of sises   ·   ·   ·   ·   .   .   xij d. ob.
Paid ser Richard Cowper, for the kepinge of a booke of
christeninges and burienges   .   .   ij s.
Paid to John Blunt, for a lader .   .   .   .   .   viij d.
Item, delivered the belle man, for a corde to the organs   ij d.
Delivered the deacon, a corde for the lantern   .   .   j d.
Paid Thomas Season, for mendinge of alle the glasse
windowes in the churche, and he to leve not one
hole in alle the windowes .   .   .   .   .   viij s.
Paid Homfry the pavier, for iij quarters servise in the
churche   .   .   .   .   iiij s.
Summa   .   .   v li. iiij s. iij d.
So rest due to the parishe   .   .   .   v li. xvj s. j d.

Receittes receyvede by Rycharde Swanson and Richard
Hucke for the use of the parishe, beinge churche
wardens.

Receyvede of the olde churche wardens, the 8. day of
November   .   .   .   .   .   .   iv li.
Received of the parisheners at Easter   .   .   .   xxxvij s. j d.
Received of the parisheners, as by quarter contributors
unto the parac'ons of the churche, as apperithe by
booke of their names   .   .   .   .   iij li. 3 s. 3 d.
Received of a straunger for a grave   .   .   .   .   vj s. viij d.
Received of Thomas Raynoldes for a grave   .   .   vj s. viij d.
Received of m^{rs} Handley for a grave   .   .   vj s. viij d.
Received of m^{rs} Pooton for a grave   .   .   .   vj s. viij d.
Received of m^{rs} Langforde for a grave   .   .   .   vj s. viij d.
Received for a pewe sett unto Thomas Raynoldes one
the northe side, late mistres Cortes   .   .   iij s. iiij d.

Received of John Merson, for half a pewe, on the southe
side, withe John Griffettes bucher . . . ij s. iiij d.
Received of Richarde Hucke, for half a pewe on the
northe side, surrendrede by m^{rs} Handley . . xij d.
Summa of alle receittes ys   xj li. iiij d.
Finis.

Reparacions donne by John Clongnas and Thomas Deos, churche wardens of Ludlow, anno Domini 1564.

In primis, the vij. day of November, in candles. . iij d.
Item, the xiiij. day of November, in candles . . iij d.
Item, the xxj. day of November, in candles . . iij d.
Item, the xxviij. day of November, in candles . . iij d.
Item, paid to William Powis, on the last day of Novem-
ber, for one pounde of sises . . . . x d.
Item, paid on the v. daye of December, for candles . iij d.
Item, the xij. day of December, for candles . . . iij d.
Item, the xix. day of December, for candles . . iij d.
Item, the xxvij. day of December, for candles . . iij d.
Item, the xxviij. day of December, to William Powes for
one pounde of sise . . . . x d.
Item, the vj. day of January, for candles . . iij d.
Item, the xv. day of January, for candles . . iij d.
Item, the xxiij. day of January, for candles . . iij d.
Item, one the last day of January, for candles . . iij d.
Item, one the viij. day of February, candles · iij d.
Item, for candles one Easter day . vj d.
Item, for j li. of sises, to William Powes . x d.
Item, more iij pounde of candles . . ix d.
Item, ij li. of candles and a pounde of tallowe ix d.
Item, to Powes for half a pounde of sise . . . v d.
Item, paid for candles the xj. of November . . xviij d.
Item, paid Richarde Swanson for cordes to hange up evy
at Christmas about the churche . . . . viij d.

Item, paid to Stephen Knyght, for mendynge the fore
    belle clapper before Christmas last .   .   .   xvj d.

Item, paid to Richarde Wodwarte, for to mende the
    chymes against Christmas in wier .   .   .   iiij d.

Item, paid to Thomas Acrue for mendinge of the baw-
    dricke to the belles against Christmas . . iij s. viij d.

Item, paid Richarde Halle, for dressinge the churche
    with yve .   .   .   .   .   .   iiij d.

Item, paid one the xiiij. daie of Marche, to the plom-
    mer, for castinge of a leven hundrede of leade . lj s. iiij d.

Item, paid to the plummer for iij skore and fyftene
    poundes of sowder for the leades .   .   . xxxvij s. vj d.

Item, paid the plumer, on the xvij. day of Aprelle, for
    vij daies worke for hym self and his man . .   xiiij s.

Item, paid to Yevan the carpenter, on the x. day of
    Februari, for layinge a pece of tymber in a sommer
    of the churche .   .   .   .   iiij d.

Item, paid for the pece of tymber and nayles . .   iiij d.

Item, paid for ij sawyde bordes .   .   .   .   xvij d.

Item, paid for ij rasters [1] .   .   .   .   .   xiiij d.

Item, paid to Thomas of Galforde, for settinge in of ij
    rasters [1] in the tope of the churche .   .   iij d.

Item, paid for nayles, for the plomer to nayle the leedes   xvj d.

Item, paid to Joyce Idwyn, for ij shemes of wode for
    the plumer .   .   .   .   .   .   viij d.

Item, paid for the carienge of the leade to the plumers
    house to cast .   .   .   .   .   .   v d.

Item, paid to the collyer for coles .   .   .   viij d.

Item, paid to the chamberleyne for a sawede borde   iiij d.

Item, paid to Watter Bolde and his man for worke .   viij d.

Item, paid to Richard Crosse, for mendinge of the locke
    of the vestrie dore, and makinge a key to the same dore   ij s.

---

[1] In the MS. it is clearly *rasters*, but the long *s* and the *f* are so nearly alike, that we cannot always distinguish them, and it may be intended for *rafters*.

Item, for mendinge of a key to the churche dore . iiij d.

Item, paid for a booke for one of the singeinge boyes . vj d.

Item, paid to John Sothern and Wodwarde for walles
on the churche house . . . . . xiiij d.

Item, for skynes,[1] glue, and alam, to mend the organs xij d.

Item, paid to the pavier, for pavinge withe in the churche
at the northe day . . . . . ij d.

Paid to Thomas Acrue, for mendinge of a bawdricke for
the secounde belle . . . . . . vj d.

Item, paid to Raffe glassier, for glassinge the churche
windowes . . . . xiiij s.

Item, paid to Rooe, for takinge downe of the belle . viij d.

Item, paid James Willes, to kepe dogges out of the
churche . . . . iiij d.

Item, paid ale and bere to John Rogers for them that
toke downe the belle . . . . . . xij d.

Item, paid for the wrytinge of our bokes . . . viij d.

Item, paid for the caryenge of a ladder from master
Barnabies house to the churche . . . ij d.

Item, paid to Steven Knyght, for mendinge a locke of
the clocke house . . . . . . ij d.

Item, paid to the deacon at iiij severalle tymes v li. vj s. viij d.

Item, paid the deacon for reparacion of the chymes vj s. viij d.

Item, paid the deacon for mendinge of the belle ropes and
storringe [2] the lantorne, and for storringe the steple
and leedes . . . . iij s. iiij d.

Item, paid ser Richarde Cowper, for kepinge the parishe
booke . . . . ij s.

Item, paid John Blunt, for mendinge the grate . . iiij d.

Summa tottallis . . xiij li. viij s. j d.

Recevid by us the saide churche wardens, at our com-
mynge into our office, the some of . . . v li. xvj s.

Item, more received of the money that was getherede
of the parishe at Easter last past . . . xxxv s.

---

[1] Probably a local word.   [2] Another word the meaning of which is obscure.

Item, more received of Robert Draper, for his mothers
    burialle in the churche   .   .   .   .   . vj s. viij d.
Item, more received of Alles Poope, for her mothers bu-
    rialle in the churche   .   .   .   .   .   . vj s. viij d.
Item, received of quarterege for the reparacion of the
    churche and the decons wages, as apperithe by bille vij li. ij d.
            Summa of alle receittes   xv li. iiij s. vj d.
    So restes due to the churche   .   .   xxxvj s. v d.

            Pewes voyde and to be sett.
            One pew late m^{rs} Bradshaw.
            A pew by the deathe of m^{rs} Draper.
            A pew by the deathe of William Tandie.

Grauntede to John Clongnas, half a pew with m^{r} Farr,
    and payde to the churche   .   .   .   . iij s. iiij d.
Grauntede to Thomas Deos and Thomas Shrawley, a
    pew rome behynde the seide pew, to bylde upon,
    and paid for the same   .   .   .   . iij s. iiij d.
Grauntede to William Pope, gent., the pew late mistres
    Bradshaw, and paid therfore   .   .   .   viij s.
            Summa   .   .   .   xiij s. viij d.
Wiche some togethor withe the forseide some of xxxvj s.
    v d. ys delyverede into thandes of the new churche
    wardens, in toto   .   .   .   .   lj s. j d.
            Finis.[1]

The accompttes of Richarde Heath and John Waties,
churche wardens from the feaste of Alle Sayntes
anno Domini 1565 unto the seide feast, for on hoole
yeare, anno Domini 1566.

In primis, paid to Richarde Handle for his yeres wages   v s. iiij d.

---

[1] After this, there are six pages of the manuscript left blank, no doubt to receive the
Churchwardens' accounts for 1565, which were never entered.

Item, to Thomas Higges, for kepinge the clocke and
    chymes .   .   .   . vj s. viij d.

Item, to mr Tanner, for mendynge the bellies of the
    great organs .   .   .   .   .   . iij s. iiij d.

Item, to John Blunt and his man, for ij. dayes worke
    on the great belle .   .   .   .   .   . ij s. x d.

Item, to Thomas Season, for ij. daies worke on the same
    belle .   .   .   . xx d.

Item, to William Hardinge for helpinge about the grett
    belle, and the hevinge up of the pese .   .   . viij d.

Item, to Stephen Knyght, for nayles and mendinge the
    buckelles to the great belle .   .   .   . xvij d.

Item, for iij. shorte bordes to leye under ther fette at the
    deske .   .   .   . viij d.

Item, for ij. barres for the grate, and settinge in of
    them .   .   .   . viij d.

Item, to James Willes, for his yeres wages .   .   . iij s. iiij d.

Item, to Richarde Haule, for hollie and yevie, and his
    candlestickes .   .   .   . viij d.

Item, to William Powes, for iiij. pounde and a halfe of
    syses candles .   .   .   .   .   . iij s. ix d.

Item, to Thomas Season, for takynge downe of the
    wedercocke, and settinge up of hit agaune .   . iiij s. viij d.

Item, in drincke .   .   .   .   .   . iiij d.

Item, to hym for ix. fote of new glasse .   .   . vij s. vj d.

Item, more to hym for vj. fote of pessinge .   .   . ij s.

Item, more to hym for the mendinge of smale holes in
    the churche windowes .   .   .   . iij s. iiij d.

Item, for ij. fote of new glasse .   .   .   . xx d.

Item, more for j. fote of pessinge .   .   . iiij d.

Item, for bandes for the windowes, and j. iron barre x d.

Item, for half a pounde of wyer .   .   .   . vj d.

Item, in paper to ser Richarde Cowper .   . ij d.

Item, for ij. barres for the grate .   .   .   . vj d.

Item, paid to John Blunt and John Rooe, for mendinge
    the bere and the grate   .   .   .   .   .   xiiij d.

Item, for nayles   .   .   .   .   .   .   iiij d.

Item, to Richarde Haule, for swepinge the glasse win-
    dowes about the churche against Easter   .   .   iiij d.

Item, to John Blunt and John Roe, for j. dayes worke
    on the secounde tenor   .   .   .   .   .   xx d.

Item, to Thomas Higges, for pessinge the belle ropes,
    and washinge the table clothes   .   .   .   .   xx d.

Item, for ij. new belle ropes to the geret belle and the
    secounde tenor .   .   .   .   x s. vj d.

Item, to Thomas a Crue for a new bawdricke   .   .   xx d.

Item, to the saide Thomas, for mendinge v. bawdrickes   ij s.

Item, to Thomas Higges for his yeres wages   .   v li. vj s. viij d.

Item, to mᵗ chauncelor, at the delyveringe of the
    christeninge boke   .   .   .   .   .   .   xij d.

Item, paid to mʳ Tanner, for mendinge of the great
    organs   .   .   .   .   xx s.

Item, to Thomas Willson, and John Luston, for mak-
    inge clenne under the grate   .   .   .   xij d.

Item, paid to John Rooe, for mendinge of the bere   .   ij s.

Item, to John Rawlyns, saddler, for tho mendinge of iij.
    bawdrickes   .   .   .   .   .   .   xiiij d.

Item, to Thomas Bedow, for a pece of tymber to make
    iij. stockes to the belle   .   .   .   .   iiij s. viij d.

Item, paid for xij. horse lodes of lyme   .   .   .   v s.

Item, for ij. cordes to the organs   .   .   .   viij d.

Item, for a belle to James Willes   .   .   .   ij d.

Item, spent gowinge to Clyfton to my lorde bishope   .   xvj d.

Item, to mʳ Parson, for a booke of prayer against the
    Torke ¹   .   .   .   .   .   .   vj d.

---

¹ The Turks were at this time threatening Europe in the East and in the Mediterranean,
and prayers were ordered to be offered up against them in parish churches all over England. In the Church Wardens' Accounts of the parish of St. Helen's, Abingdon, the

Item, to Hoelle Smythe, for a lode of sande . . . viij d.

Item, to Crokett, for dyginge and siftinge of ytt, and
for a new rydle · . . . . . iiij d.

Item, paid to Richard Hobbie, for mendinge of the grate viij d.

Item, to Steven Knyght, for shuttinge of the springes of
the chymes, and for a clampe of iron for naylles,
and for v neue nottes . . . . . ij s. iiij d.

Item, paid for xx li. of tallow candles, delivered to the
deacon . . . . v s.

Item, paid to Walter Boulde, for mendynge of the but-
tresses about the churche . . . . ij s. viij d.

      Summa . . xj li. vij s. viij d.

Receyvede for burialles in the churche.

Received for the burialle of William Benson . . vj s. viij d.

Received for the burialle of John a Gwillm . . vj s viij d.

Received for the burialle of m^{rs} Walker . . . vj s. viij d.

Memorandum, received for the Easter duties . . xlij s.

    Item, that we have sett these setes folowinge.

In primis, to Symonde Thorton and Jane his wif, on
sette on the southe side of the churche, which was
m^{rs} Foxe . . . . iiij s.

Item, one sette to Thomas Alsope and Agnes his wyf,
and Thomas Hunte and Elsabeth hys wif, wiche
was Edwarde Cuppers . . . . iiij s.

Item, to William Cleobury, on seate on the northe syde
the weddinge churche dore, which was Ancrete
Beadoes . . . . ix s. vj d.

Item, on sete to Richarde Cupper, baker, and Elynor his
wife, one the northe side the foute, which was William Pensons . . . . vj s.

following entry occurs: " Anno 1565, payde for two bookes of common prayer agaynste
invading of the Turke, vj d." Sixpence appears to have been the established price of this
book of prayer.

Item, on sette to Richarde Heathe and Elynor his wife,
sett on the northe syde the poore mans boxe, wiche
was Thomas Raskolles, at .   .   .   .   .   v s. viij d.

Item, on sette to Elsabeth Bottfylde, on the northe syde
the churche, adyoyninge to on of the arches, wich
was Davie Jones   .   .   .   .   .   xx d.

Item, on half sete to John Dalton and Jane his wife,
parte with mistres Partrige, wiche was old m^{res}
Drapers, at   .   .   .   .   .   ij s.

Item, on sete to Morris Philipes and Agnes his wife,
beinge benethe the deske, and nowe in the tenure
of the saide Morrice Philipes, at   .   .   .   iij s.

         Summa .   .   .   iiij li. xviij s. x d.
         Sum of the hole charge .   .   .   xj li. xvij s. vj d.
         Whereof payde .   .   .   .   xj li. vij s. viij d.
So the churche wardens rest in the churches dett   ix s. x d.
Whereof paid to the deacon for settinge clocke and chymes vj s. viij d.
         Payde therof to ser Richarde Cupper .   .   ij s.
         So restes .   .   .   .   ij s. x d.
         Finis.

The accomptes of Thomas Ashbage and Henry Cleoburie, churche wardens of the towne of Ludlow, anno Domini 1567.

Item, paid to Thomas Higges, beinge deacon, for one
yeres wages .   .   .   .   .   .   v li. vj s. viij d.

Item, paid to Richarde Haule, for one yeres wages .   v s. iiij d.

Item, paid to hym for the hanginges aboute the churche
at Christmas .   .   .   .   .   .   viij d.

Item, paid for ij. belle ropes for the seconde tenor and
our Lady belle .   .   .   .   .   .   x s. vj d.

Item, paid for one gable rope for the chymes and one
rope for the mornynge prayer belle .   .   viij s. viij d.

Item, paid Thomas Season, for xxxiiij. li. of leade at ij d.
the li.   .   .   .   .   .   .   v s. viij d.

Item, paid to hym for xij li. soder, at vij d. the pounde   vij s.

Item, for rossen and nayles to the same worke   .   .   ij d.

Item, paid to Thomas Season, for vj. daies worcke for
hym and his boye in the monethe of Marche   .   vj s.

Item, paid to Thomas Season, for iiij li. of soder in the
monethe of October . . . . . .   ij s. iiij d.

Item, paid to Thomas Season, for one dayes worcke and
a half for hym and his boye, in the moneth of October . . . .   xvj d.

Item, paid to Walter Boulde, in Marche, for a xj. dayes
worke and a halfe, at xij d. the day   .   .   .   xj s. vj d.

Item, paid to William Lloyde, laborer, for x dayes worke
in the monethe of Marche, at vj d. the daye   .   v s.

Item, paid for viij. bozells of lyme, and one rynge ¹ of
tanners lyme, in Marche last   .   .   .   iij s.

Item, paid to Howelle Smythe, for on lode of sande and
the syftinge of the same   .   .   .   .   viij d.

Item, paid for on pece of tymber for the ruffe ² of the
churche on the southe side .   .   .   .   iij d.

Item, paid Walter Boulde, for the makynge a pece for
the chyme, and Edwarde Humffries, his servantt,
to helpe hym   .   .   .   .   .   .   ix d.

Item, paid for coles and faggottes to heate the plumers
yercons ³ .   .   .   .   xix d.

Item, paid to James Cowerne, for his paynes in com-
mynge to vewe ⁴ the steple .   .   .   .   xij d.

Item, paid to James Wylles, for the fachinge ⁵ of the for-
saide James Cowerne .   .   .   .   .   iiij d.

Item, delivered unto the deacon in paste candles ⁶ xviij li.
at iij d. the pounde   .   .   .   .   .   iiij s. vj d.

Item, delivered to the deacon v li. and half of syses   .   iiij s. vij d.

¹ A name for a measure or quantity which I have not met with elsewhere.
² Roof.   ³ Irons.   ⁴ To view, examine.
⁵ Fetching.   ⁶ Perhaps we should read *Passe* (i.e. Easter) *candles*.

Item, paid to John Trueman and Richard Johnson, for
  the pryckeinge oute of synginge bokes . . xiiij s.
Item, paid to Lewys the tyler and Thomas Wilson, for
  makinge cleane of the churche windowes and the
  walles . . . . ij s. vj d.
Item, paid Thomas a Crue for one bauld rope . . xx d.
Item, paid John Rawlyns, sadler, for the mendinge of
  ij. bauld ropes [1] . . . . . . viij d.
Item, paid John Roe, carpender, for the makinge of
  new lokers, and for mendinge of grates in the
  church calendes . . . . . . ij s. iiij d.
Item, paid John Rooe, for the mendinge of the bere ij d.
Item, paid John Dallton, for a Psallter boke . . ij s.
Item, paid for ij. coordes to the organs . . . iiij d.
Item, paid Thomas Season, for hanginge of the lampe
  and fastenynge of the glasse in the steple . . viij d.
Item, paid to Raffe Harvie, for xxxviij. foote of new
  glasse, at ix d. the foote . . . . xxviij s. vj d.
Item, paid to the said Raffe, for the settinge up of xiiij.
  foote of olde glasse, at iij d. the foote . . . iij s. vj d.
Item, paid to Thomas Season, for xxx. foote of new
  glasse, at ix d. the foote . . . . . xxij s. vj d.
Item, paid to Thomas Season, for the settinge up of
  xxxiij. foote of olde glasse, at iij d. the foote . viij s. vj d.
Item, paid to Richarde Crosse, for v. staffpes [2] for the
  glasse windowes in the stepulle . . . xij d.
Item, to hym for one claspe of yron more for the whele
  of the belle . . . . vj d.
Item, for on lesser claspe of yron . . . . ij d.
Item, for clyppes of yron to the bere . . . . ij d.
Item, for on key to a cooffer in the highe chauncelle . iij d.

---

[1] What are elsewhere called *baldricks*.

[2] This word is written rather confusedly; and I am not sure it was not intended to be *staples*, or perhaps *clasps*.

Item, paid to Steven Knyght for v. claspes of iron to
the arches of the churche, wiche Walter Boulde
dyde mende, on the southe syde . . . . ij s. iij d.

Item, paid to Steven Knyght, for the mendinge of the
greate belle clapper, at ij. severalle tymes . . vj s.

Item, paid unto Stephen, for xvj. nayles, and for settinge on a claspe on the stocke of the belle . . vj d.

Item, paid for the makinge of our boke to gether our
quartereges by . . . . viij d.

Item, paid to the deacon, for the kepinge of the clocke
and the chymes . . . . . . vj s. viij d.

Item, paid Thomas Higges, deacon, for pesynge the belle
ropes at sondry tymes . . . . . xvj d.

Summa totallis disbursed . . xiiij li. xiiij s. iiij d.

Memorandum, receyvede by Thomas Ashebache and Henry Cleoburie to the use of the parishe.

Receyvede at the handes of Richarde Heath and John
Watties of the stocke of the churche . . . x d.

Item, received of the Easter boke in money . . xl s.

Received of the inhabitauntes dwellynge in the towne
of Ludlow, for quarterege . . . . vj li. xiij s. x d.

Received, for ij. burialles in the churche, on for m^{res}
Belle thelder, and the other for William Wattes
syster . . . . xiij s. iiij d.

Received of Richarde Maddokes, for grounde to byld on
pew at the nether arche . . . . . ij s.

Received of m^r Farre, for half a pew wiche John
Clongnas did assine over to hym . . . xviij d.

Received of John Moriys, wever, for halfe a pew that
Richarde Adams wife, his mother-in-law, assignede
over to hym . . . . ij s. iiij d.

Received of Henry Cleoburie, for on pew graunted to
hym by John Sherman, gent., and William Yo-
mans, then beinge baylyfes of Ludlow   .   .   iij s iiij d.
Received of Watter Taylor, tanner, for the rent of the
bricke closse due at Mychalmas   .   .   .   viij s.
    Summa   .   .   x li. v s. ij d.
  So the parishe resteth in the churche wardens dett
  for this yeare .   .   .   iiij li. ix s. ij d.
     Finis.

A just accomptt made by me, George Sothern and John
Belle, churche wardens of Ludlow, then bayliffes
Robert Leues and Edwarde Bager, anno Domini
1568.

In primis, unto Richarde Haule, for his yeares wages, for
blowynge of the organs and kepinge of the churche
clene   .   .   .   .   v s. iiij d.
Item, paid to Thomas Iligges, for his hole yeares
wages   .   .   .   .   v li. vj s. viij d.
Item, paid to John Rooe, for ij. bordes to make wether
bordes for the windowes in the steple   .   .   xviij d.
Item, paid unto the same John Rooe, for the workinge
of the same bordes, for on dayes worke   .   .   vj d.
Item, paid to John Sawiere, his servante, for the same
dayes workes withe hym   .   .   .   .   .   iiij d.
Item, paid for ij. cordes for the organs   .   .   .   iij d.
Item, paid for clote neales to neale a plate of yron of
one of the belle whilles   .   .   .   .   .   j d.
Item, paid to Raffe, glacier, for the glasinge of the
window in saynt Margrettes chauncelle   .   .   iiij s. x d.
Item, paid to Richarde Haule, for yeves and hollies for
the churche   .   .   .   .   vj d.
Item, paid to Thomas Season, for tornynge of the clocke
on the secounde tenor   .   .   .   .   .   xij d.

Item, paid to Thomas Cruc, for the lyninge of baw-
dickes . . . . viij d.

Item, paid to Thomas Season, for sowder for the leades
of the churche on the northe side . . . iij s.

Item, halfe a pounde of rossen . . . . . j d.

Item, paid for bordes . . . . . . ij d.

Item, paid for woode to heate the irons . . . ij d.

Item, paid to James Willes, for drivinge doges out of
the churche . . . . ij s. iiij d.

Item, paid to Thomas Season, for makinge clene the stiple iiij s.

Item, paid to Thomas Season, for workinge of the leades ij s. vj d.

Item, paid to John Blunt and his man, for hanginge
the secounde tenor . . . . . . xx d.

Item, paid to Richarde Crosse, for makinge ij. peare of
buckels for the secounde tenor, and for makinge
naylles to neale the same buckles . . . xix d.

Item, paid for ij. seses and a lode of sande . . x d.

Item, paid to John Rawlyns, for a bawdricke for the
fore belle . . . . vj d.

Item, paid Water Bolde, for iij. dayes worke on the
churche walle . . . . iij s.

Item, paid to John Erle . . . . . . iij s. iiij d.

Item, paid to John Reynaldes . . . . . xviij d.

Item, paid for poles and bordes to make the cather [1] for
the steple . . . . xij d.

Item, paid for lyme . . . . vj s. iij d.

Item, paid for nayles . . . . . xiiij d.

Item, paid for viij. haulters . . . . . viij d.

Item, paid for ij. knotes [2] of cordes . . . . xvj d.

Item, paid to Howelle Smythe, for ij. lode of sande carienge . . . . viij d.

Item, paid to Crokett, for the siftinge of ytt . . iiij d.

---

[1] Another word of doubtful meaning. In the dialects of the North of England a *cather*
is a cradle.   [2] ? knots.

Item, paid for one lode of poles   .   .   .   **xxij d.**

Item, paid for a rynge   .   .   .   .   .   **xxij d.**

Item, paid to Watter Bolde, for workinge one the steple
xix dayes, havinge xvj d. a day   .   .   **xxv s. iiij d.**

Item, paid to Thomas Season, for workinge one the
steple xix. dayes, havinge xj d. a day   .   .   **xvij s. v d.**

Item, paid to John Sawier, for workinge one the steple
xix. dayes, havinge vj d. a day   .   .   .   .   **ix s. vj d.**

Item, paid to John Renaldes, for workinge one the
steple xx. dayes, havinge vij d. a day   .   .   .   **xj s. j d.**

Item, paid to John Erle, for workinge one the steple
xiiij. dayes, havinge xij d. a day   .   .   .   **xiiij s.**

Item, paid to Watter Bolde, for makinge of a cradelle to
goe about the steple   .   .   .   .   .   **xij d.**

Item, paid to Steven Knyght, for workynge of xxvj.
pounde and a halufe of iron, withe ij pounde and a
halfe of his owne, at iij. ferthinges a pounde workynge   .   .   .   .   **iiij s. vj d.**

Item, paid for a pounde of candles to Water Bolde, to
see to worke in the chyme lofte   .   .   .   **iij d.**

Item, paid to Thomas Season, for xij. pounde of leade   **xviij d.**

Item, paid for ale into the stiple at the takinge downe
of the belle   .   .   .   .   .   .   **xvj d.**

Item, for packethirde and whipcorde   .   .   .   **iij d.**

Item, to William, torner, for turnynge of the powleys   **ij d.**

Item, for lycar for the same powleys   .   .   .   **iiij d.**

Item, paid to Humfry Season, for one dayes worke at
the takynge downe of the belle   .   .   .   **viij d.**

Item, paid to Richarde Season, for one dayes worke at
the takinge downe of the belle   .   .   .   **vj d.**

Item, paid to John Blunt, for ij. dayes worke for stock-
inge and hanginge of the belle   .   .   .   **ij s.**

Item, paid to Thomas Season, for ij. dayes at the hanginge up of the belle   .   .   .   .   .   **ij s.**

Item, paid to Frances the belle fonder, for hanginge up
  of the belle   .   .   .   .   iij s.
Item, paid to Humfry Ley, for wyer for the chymes   iiij d.
Item, paid for a pece of tymber for the steple   .   .   xij d.
Item, paid for a pottelle of wyne, when we went to m^r
  Hopton to borow hys gable [1]   .   .   .   viij d.
Item, paid for a horse to carie the same gable   .   .   iiij d.
Item, paid to John Blunt for ij. dayes for the grate for
  the churche yearde   .   .   .   .   .   .   viij d.
Item, delivered to Thomas Higges in talow candles, ix
  pounde at iij d. and iij d. ob. a pounde, and for iij.
  pounde and a quarter of a pounde of waxe candles,
  beinge at x d. a pounde   .   .   .   .   .   v s. iij d.
Item, delivered to Richarde Haule, iij. pounde of candles
  at Christmas last, to set in the body of the churche   ix d.
Item, paid to John Erle for the coveringe of ij. graves   vj d.
Item, paid for a rope for the fore belle   .   .   .   iiij s. vj d.
Item, paid to Steven Knyght, for a plate for one of the
  belle whiles   .   .   .   .   vj d.
Item, more to Steven Knyght, for mendinge of the
  chyme   .   .   .   .   ij d.
Item, paid to the smythe of Ludfort for the stable of the
  gret belle   .   .   .   .   ij s. viij d.
Item, paid to ser Richard Cowper for the kepinge of
  the register booke   .   .   .   .   .   ij s.
Item, paid to Crue for mendinge of a bawdricke   .   iiij d.
Item, paid to John Blunt for mendinge ij. callans [2]   .   vj d.
Item, paid to Crue for makinge a bawdricke for the
  grett belle   .   .   .   .   ij s.
Item, more to hym for mendinge ij. bawdrickes for ij.
  of the least belles   .   .   .   .   .   .   iiij d.

---

[1] *i.e.* cable.
[2] The meaning of this seems rather obscure. Perhaps it means the two callends, or lichegates, the principal one, and that of the College, mentioned before.

Item, paid for lij. pounde of iron, at j d. ob. the pounde
to Steven Knyght . . . . vj s. vj d.

Item, paid for the workinge of xlij. pounde, at iij. quarter
the pounde . . . . ij s. vj d.

Item, paid to William Season, for workinge xix dayes
one the steple . . . . vj s. viij d.

Item, paid to Thomas Higges for one pounde of candles   iij d. ob.

Item, delivered more to Thomas Higges, one pounde of
waxe candles . . . . x d.

Item, to Richarde Crosse for a while to the chymes .   xvj d.

Item, paid more to Crosse for shuttinge the springe that
berethe the clocke hamer . . . . . ij d.

Item, mor to Crosse for shuttinge the whope of the
stocke of the yelde [1] belle . . . . . j d.

Item, for one of the keys for the chymes for the mendinge of ytt . . . . j d.

Item, paid for the mendinge of the staye of the wache
while . . . . j d.

Item, paid for vj. pound of iron, and for the makinge
of the claper for the yelde belle . . . . ij s. vj d.

Item, paid for the workinge of iij. score pounde of iron
for the hanginge up of the yelde belle . . . iij s. iiij d.

Item, paid to master Beeke for iiij. lodes of lyme .   ij s.

Item, paid to Thomas Season for the coveringe of
Annes Tranter grave . . . . . iiij d.

Item, paid to Thomas Powelle, carpenter, for the mendinge of the churche grate . . . . . vj d.

Item, delivered to Higges one pounde of candles .   iij d. ob.

Item, more to Lanfilde the barber, for one pounde of waxe
candles . . . . x d.

Item, paid to Watter Bolde, for the coveringe of ij. graves   viij d.

Item, paid for ij. lynkes for the churche . . . xiiij d.

Sum tottallis of this allowaunce . xv li. xix s.

[1] Guild bell.

Receyvede for the burialles in the churche.

In primis, received of John Philipes, alles Capper, for the
    burialle of his mother   .   .   .   .   . vj s. viij d.
Item, received for the burialle of m^r Walters man   . vj s. viij d.
Item, received for the burialle of on Pyxley, that diede
    at master Stringer house   .   .   .   .   . vj s. viij d.
Item, received for the burialle of John Handmere, m^r
    Gerrades man   .   .   .   . vj s. viij d.
Item, received for the burialle of Aggnes Traunter   .   vj s. viij d.
Item, received for the burialle of William Hucke wife   vj s. viij d.

Receyvede for pues.

In primis, received of William Frenche, baker, for one
    pew one the southe side against saynt Cathern
    chauncelle .   .   .   . v s.
Item, received of John Phillipes, ales Capper, for haulfe
    a pewe on the northe side against saynt Margrettes
    chauncelle .   .   .   . iiij s.

Receyvede in money at Easter.

Item, receyvede at Easter for the Easter booke   .   .   xlij s.
Getherede for the reparacon of the churche and the dea-
    cons wages of the parishe this some as here after
    folowith   .   .   .   . vj li. v s. iiij d.
            Sum of the receittes   .   . x li. xvj s. iiij d.
So rest due to the churche wardens uppon this ac-
    comptt   .   .   .   . v li. ij s. viij d.
Wherof receyvede of master Passie for the after marthe [1]
    of Portman meadow, [2] wiche ought to be commen,
    savinge the order   .   .   .   .   .   . vj s. viij d.
                Finis.

[1] After-math.
[2] Portman meadow is mentioned in all the churchwardens' accounts about this period.
It appears that it was leased to Mr. Passie, and that some disagreement had arisen about it.

VILLA DE   The account of William Browne and Thomas
LUDLOW.   Shrawley, churchewardens, in the tyme of
           Richarde Farr and John Taylor, bayliffes,
           vz. anno Domini 1569.

In primis, payd unto Thomas Higges, being deacon, ffor
    his whole yeres wages .   .   .   .   v li. vj s. viij d.
Item, payd unto Richard Halle for his ffee in the churche
    ffor the whole yere .   .   .   .   .   .   v s. iij d.
Item, payd unto Jamys Willes ffor his fee ffor whipping
    of dogges out of churche .   .   .   .   .   iij s.
Item, payd unto Richard Hall for holly and evy against
    Christmas, to hang in the church .   .   .   vj d.
Item, paid unto Richard Swanson ffor ij°. belles ffor the
    whip to whip dogges out of church .   .   .   iiij d.
Item, deliveryd to Richard Halle iij. li. of candelles to
    burne in the churche one Christmas day .   .   ix d.
Item, payd unto Steven Knight, ffor shutting and mend-
    ing of the clapper of the santes bell .   .   .   iiij d.
Item, payd ffor the top or cover of the beer, ffor the
    mendinge of the same, and naylles .   .   .   ij d.
Item, payd unto Thomas Season, ffor mendinge of the
    fount in manor and fforme folowing, viz.: ffor wood
    ij d., ffor workemanship ij d., ffor sowerder [1] vj d.   in all x d.
Item, payd unto Steven Knight ffor mending of the
    second clapper, and making him shorter .   .   vj d.
Item, payd ffor wier ffor the mending of the chymes .   iiij d.
Item, iij. smale cordes ffor the glasier to bynd his ladders   ij d.
Item, payd for iij°. keyes and ij°. haspes and naylles ffor
    ij°. coffers in the high chaunsell .   .   .   .   ix d.
Item, ffor mending of the beer at ij. severall tymes, a
    claspe of iron, in nalles and workemanship .   xj d.

                    [1] Soder.

Item, payd ffor xvj. li. of tallow candelles at severall
tymes, deliveryd to the deacon, at 3 d. the pound   iiij s.

Item, iiij. li. of sizes at severall tymes, deliveryd to the
deacon . . . . iij s. iiij d.

Item, payd unto Thomas Season, ffor the covering of
Richard Tomlyns grave . . . . . iij d.

Item, payd unto Thomas Season, ffor the covering of
John Benyons grave . . . . . . iij d.

Item, payd unto Season ffor the covering of Walter
Taylors wieffes grave . . . . . . iij d.

Item, payd unto Thomas Season ffor the mending of
severall places, as paving in the northe yle of the
church . . . . iij d.

Item, payd ffor the mending of the second belle whele
and naylles . . . . ij d.

Item, payd unto Raffe Harvye, ffor vij^en ffoote of newe
glasse in St. Margettes chaunsell, at 8 the foote   iiij s. viij d.

More to him, ffor setting of xj. ffoote of old glasse in
the same chauncell, at 3 d. the ffoote . . ij s. ix d.

Item, payd ffor iij. long sawede bordes ffor to make a
dore into the vestery . . . . . . ij s.

Item, payd unto the masson ffor the breking of the
wawle and ffashioning of the dore in the vestery, ffor
him and his man, by the agreementes of m^r bayliffes   iiij s. vj d.

Item, payd unto John Blunt and his man, ffor ij^o. dayes
work in making of the dore in the vesterye . . ij s. iiij d.

Item, payd ffor viij li. of lead, to faste the hokes of the
vestery dore in the walle . . . . . xij d.

Item, payd unto Steven Knight, ffor workmanship of
xxxvj li. of old iron wich was in the vestry window
before, as foloweth, viz. ij^o. gret hinges, ij^o. hokes,
ij^o. boltes, iiij^or. staples, xliiij^or. grete naylles. . iiij s. vj d.

Item, payd more ffor iiij li. of wast iron, in exchang in
the same iron . . . . . . vj d.

Item, in spicke nayles ffor the same dore . . . ix d.

Item, payd ffor the making cleane of the said vestry,
and of the sayd kreking [1] of stones and ramell . iij d.

Item, payd ffor the mending of the gabulle rope of the
chymes, to Thomas Higges . . . . viij d.

Item, payd ffor the iron and making of ij. hokes to claspe
the clocke howse unto the wawle . . . viij d.

Item, payd ffor iiij li. of lead to fasten the sayd hokes into
the wall . . . . vj d.

Item, payd ffor the setting in of the sayd ij°. hokes, and
making of the holles into the walle, and a handell
ffor the thrid belle, and naylles . . . . xij d.

Item, payd unto Fraunces Bellingham, the bell-fownder,
and Thomas Season, ffor trussing of the grete belle,
being lose in the stocke, and moving the brasses. xvj d·

Item, payd unto the smithe ffor viij. grete naylles ffor
the trussing of the same belle . . . . iiij d.

Item, payd unto Thomas Season, ffor setting a pece in
the sille for the chyme hamber at the second belle,
in timber, workmanship, and nayles . . . viij d.

Item, payd unto Thomas Season towardes his yeres
wages ffor glassing . . . . . . xx s.

Item, payd unto Steven Knight, ffor the mending of
the watchwhele of the clock . . . . viij d.

Item, payd unto John Dalton for iiij°ʳ. pricke song bokes
in printe, ffor the churche . . . . viij s.

Item, payd for the exchange of a new Bible, to John
Dalton . . . . xx s.

Item, payd unto ser Richard Cowper, ffor a coppy of
the rejester booke of the parishe of Ludlowe, con-
teigning weddinges, christninges, and burienges, in
yeres last past, to be delivderyd unto the bishop at
his visitacon, the furst of June 1569 . . . ij s.

[1] A word of which I cannot give the meaning.

Item, payd ffor the quarterege boke . . . . viij d.

Item, payd ffor iij. sawed bordes to make the gate to the
    churchyard next the almeshouse . . . . ij s.

A pece of tymber to make the same gate . . . viij d.

For bord naylles to the same gate . . . . iij d.

Item, payd ffor ij°. sawed bordes to make a gresses [1] to
    sett under the singing mens ffeete in the highe
    chaunsell . . . . xij d.

Item, borde naylles ffor the same . . . . iiij d.

For the ledges and workmanship . . . . x d.

Item, payd ffor a rope ffor the thrid bell . . iiij s. viij d.

Item, payd ffor a rope ffor the first bell . . iiij s. viij d.

Payd ffor the carriadg of the same rope ffrom Beaudley iiij d.

Item, payd ffor xxiiij. li. of iron to make barres ffor the
    windowes in saint Margerettes chauncell and other
    places . . . . iij s.

Deliveryd to Richard Hall a cord ffor the grete organes ij d.

Item, payd ffor the mending of the pullis of the chymes ij d.

Item, payd ffor the coppyeng of a book at the chaun-
    celors visitacon . . . . vj d.

Item, payd ffor the mending of the clothe over the or-
    gaynes, to Thomas Higges . . . . . v d.

Item, payd ffor the taking out of the signe of the crosse
    out of an alter clothe, to Higges wief . . . ij d.

Item, payd unto William Lloide, ffor making holles ffor
    the boltes in the vestry dore and steple dore . ij d.

Item, in takes [2] to mend the vanes of the chymes, and
    also the hundelles [3] with lethers ffor the ropes . j d.

Item, to Richard Hall, a rope ffor the smale organs . j d.

Item, to mr Far, ffor the coppieng a bok to the visi-
    tacon of the bishop . . . . . . xij d.

Item, deliveryd more withe bok of christninges and
    burienges to the chauncelors man . . . xij d.

---

[1] Low benches to stand on.   [2] Tacks.   [3] Perhaps for *handelles*.

Item, payd ffor iij. bordes for the over dore in the steple,
and ffor wetherbordes in the steple windowes   .   ij s.

Item, naylles ffor the same dore and windowes   .   .   vj d.

Item, one peyer of hinges ffor the same dore   .   .   vj d.

For a dayes work to Thomas ap Powell ffor the sayd
dore, and mending the grate   .   .   .   x d.

Item, to Richard Hall, a cord ffor the grete orgaines   ij d.

Item, grete tackes to mend the whele of the second bell   j d.

Item, payd unto one to healp aboutes the handelles and
peces of the clock and chimes   .   .   .   .   vj d.

Item, payd unto Steven Knyght, ffor making of ij°.
claspes of iron ffor the cest [1] in the almes howses   iij d.

Item, more to Steven Knight, ffor the workmanship of
xxiiij li. of iron ffor barres in the windowes in St.
Margettes chauncell, and other windowes   .   .   ij s.

Item, payd more to Steven Knight, ffor mending the
clapper of the grete bell   .   .   .   .   .   xvj d.

Item, payd unto Steven Knight, ffor xviij li. of iron to
the gate in the churchyard   .   .   .   .   ij s. iij d.

For workmanship of the same in hinges and hokes   .   xviij d.

Item, payd unto Thomas Season and one with him, upon
sowdering the leades of the churche, ffor vij°ⁿ dayes
woork, after the rate of x d. the daye ffor him self,
to the some of   .   .   .   .   v s. x d.

Item, ffor his man vij°ⁿ. dayes after vj d. a daye   .   iij s. vj d.

Item, payd ffor iij. seames of wood   .   .   .   xij d.

Item, payd ffor xij li. of sowder   .   .   .   vj s.

Item, payd to the same Thomas Season ffor ij°. dayes
pointing one the leades   .   .   .   .   xx d.

Item, payd unto Thomas Dyke, for ij. dayes pointing one
the leades   .   .   .   .   .   .   xx d.

Item, payd ffor vj. ringes [2] of lyme   .   .   .   ij s.

---

[1] Chest.   [2] Probably a local name of a measure.

Item, payd unto Thomas Season, ffor the trussing of
our Lady bell, and ij°. men with him, and ffor
other necessarys aboutes the belles . . . ij s.

Item, payd ffor naylles and shutting of the brases to the
same bell . . . . iij d.

Item, ffor a clasp of iron to the thrid bell . . iiij d.

Item, naylles ffor the same . . . j d.

Item, ffor the removing of a grave stone, and setting
in the brasse in the middle yle of the church . xvj d.

Item, a locker and a handell ffor the second bell . iiij d.

Item, payd ffor bordes to ley under the gutter over the
deacons chamber, and nayles ffor the same . vij d.

Item, payd more to Thomas Season, ffor making cleane
of the leades over all the church . . . xij d.

Item, payd unto the persons undernamed by m^r bayllifes
appointment, according to the statute for misse
heades, rattes heades, and crowes heades, as fol-
owethe [1]

Item, payd unto Richard Swanson, ffor ij°. dosen of myse
heades, the iij. of February, 1569 . . . ij d.

Item, payd unto Richard Swanson, the 19 of Februarye,
1569, ffor ij. dosen of myse heades . . ij d.

Item, payd unto Richard Swanson, the 6 of Aprill, 1569,
ffor iiij dosen of myse heades . . . iiij d.

Item, payd to John Mathewes sonne, ffor j. dosen of
myse heades . . . . . . j d.

Item, payd unto Richard Swanson, the 17 of Marche,
1569, ij. dosen of myse heades . . . ij d.

Item, to Steven Knightes sonne, ffor ix krowes heades,
in February, 1569 . . . . . iij d.

---

[1] The statute alluded to was that of 8 Elizabeth, chap. 15, " An Act for preservation
of grain," by which the churchwardens in every parish, with other persons to the number
of six, were directed to provide for the destruction of " noyfull fowles and vermyn," and
a price was set upon their heads. A numerous list of the birds and vermin thus pro-
scribed will be found in the Act.

Item, payd unto Steven Knyghtes sonne, for ij dosen of
myse heades in Marche . . . . .   ij d.

Item, payd unto Richard Swanson the iiij. of May, ffor
one dosen of myse heades . . . .   j d.

Item, payd unto m^r Smithes sonne of Crednyll, ffor iij.
yong crowes heades . . . . . .   j d.

Item, the xvj. of May, iij. crowes heades of m^r Barnabes
sonne . . . .   j d.

Item, payd unto Richard Swanson, the 16 of May, ij.
dosen of myse heades . . . .   ij d.

Item, payd unto m^r Beekes man, the 28 of May, 1569,
ffor vj chohes [1] heades . . . . .   j d.

Item, payd unto Richard Swanson, the iij. of September, j dosen of myse heades . . . .   j d.

Item, payd unto Thomas Crew, ffor mending ij. bau-
derickes of the belles at severall tymes . .   xij d.

Item, payd unto Thomas Wilson, ffor breking downe
the stones in St. Margeretes chauncell and our Lady
chauncell, that images stode upon .. . .   iiij d.

Item, payd unto Thomas Wilson, ffor the plaistering of
the same walles that the stones weere broken out,
and lyme ffor the same . . . . .   ij d.

Item, payd ffor carriage away of the broken stones, and
making cleane the chauncelles . . . .   ij d.

Item, payd unto the turner, ffor the mending the pullis
of the chymes . . . .   ij d.

Item, deliveryd to Thomas Higges, the ixth of this December, a j li. of tallow candelles, and halfe a pownd of sizes   viij d.

Item, in spick nayles to make up the gate in the churche-
yard . . . .   iij d.

Item, payd more unto Thomas Season towardes his
waiges ffor one yere, ended at All Sainctes last   xiij s. iiij d.

Item, payd unto John Dalton, ffor ij^o. Salter bookes ffor
the churche . . . . . .   v s.

[1] Choughs.

Item, payd unto John Blunt, ffor tymber at the gate in
the churchyerd . . . . viij d.

Item, payd unto John Blunt ffor the mending and reis-
ing of the brasse of the thrid bell, and setting her
upright in the brasse . . . . . . viij d.

More payd to the deacon ffor his ffee ffor mending of the
clock and chymes, wiers, and ropes . . . vj s. viij d.

More payd to sir Richard Cowper, clark, ffor keping
the book of weddinges, christninges, and burienges ij s.

Receiptes to the use of the churche as folowethe, 1569.

Imprimis, receaved at Ester . . . . . xl s.

Item, receaved of quarterege . . . . vj li. iiij s. ij d.

Item, receaved ffor the buriall of Richard Tomlyns . vj s. viij d.

Item, receaved ffor the buriall of one John Benion . vj s viij d.

Receaved ffor the buriall of Walter Taylor's wief . vj s. viij d.

Receaved ffor the buriall of mr Ellys daughter . . vj s. viij d.

Memorandum, that Elizabethe Parkys, widow, hathe
surrendred her parte of a pewe in the northe parte
of the churche to William Prikett, the 19 of February, 1569. Receaved . . . . . xvj d.

Item, receaved of Nichalas Chirme and Adam Heywood,
ffor the surrender of a pewe in the northe syde of
the churche, ffrom Thomas Reynoldes by mr bayliffes consent . . . . ij s.

Item, a pew graunted by mr bayliffes to Cutwallater ap
Edward, Auncell Clee, Ales Norton, Margaret
Norton, and Margery Norton, and to every of them,
which pewe was one Katherin Norton, deceassed,
with one yered[1] of grownd more enlarged. Receaved
ffor the same . . . . iij s iiij d.

Receaved of Richard Hill, walker,[2] ffor half a pewe one
the southe side of the church . . . . iij s. iiij d.

[1] One yard.   [2] A walker meant a fuller.

Memorandum, that Richard Lloide hathe resined a pewe in the lower end of the churche, anont [1] the font, to Thomas Shrauley, being one of the church-wardens, and to Edward ap Davith, and that wee have payd to the church therfore . . . . iij s. j d.

Item, receaved ffor certen peces of old timber bordes, taken ffrom the ffrount of sainct Johns chauncell, serving but ffor smale purpos . . . . vij s. iiij d.

Item, graunted a pew grownd ffor Robert Stringer, at our Lady chauncell dore, wherfore receaved by the consent of m^r bayliffes . . . . . iij s. iiij d.

Item, a pew graunted to m^r Poughenell, nere to the chauncell, that m^r bayliffes commenly use to knele in, graunted by the consentes of m^r bayliffes, the which pew was m^r Richarde Langfordes, decessed. Receaved . . . . ij s.

Memorandum, graunted unto Edward Acheley, one pew next adjoigning to a pew of Peter Benson, in the nether end of the southe yle of the churche, and payd ffor the same, in consideracon that m^r Blashe-feld and m^r Beck did allege hit was payd ffor be-fore, and recorded by the assigment of Joyse Edwyn . . . . vj d.

Ther is noe reversion to be graunted by the custome.
Item, receaved of Richard Dier ffor the assigment of half a pewe in the middle of the churche, ffrom John Dalton, and late his mother in lawes, by con-sent of the bayliffes . . . . . . xij d.

Receaved of m^r Passye, ffor the after mathe of Portman meadow, which ought to be commen, by order . vj s. viij d.

Item, receaved of Richard Farr and John Taylor, ffor the assigment of a pew in the middle of the churche, ffrom Richard Dier and his wief, by consentes, in money . . . . . . vj d.

Item, receaved of Richard Farr and John Taylor, ffor
the assigment of a pewe in the north syde of the
churche, from William Chelmick thelder, by
consentes . . . . vj d.

Item, receaved of William Chelmick, ffor thassigment of
half a pewe in the lower ende of the churche, ffrom
Richard Farr, being late m^r Hudsons, by consent vj d.

Item, receaved of John Dalton, ffor thassigment of a
pewe one the southe syde of the churche, ffrom
Richard Farr . . . . vj d.

VILLA DE   The accomptes of Symon Huddy and John
LUDLOW.   Rawlinges, churchwardens, in the tyme
of William Poughnill, gent. and Morres
Philipes, bayliffes, anno Domini 1570.

Inprimis to the deacon, his wages for three quarters
of the year, after xxvj s. viij d. the quarter . . iiij li.

Item, paid to Season, for his yeres wages, ended at Michaelmas, for repayringe of the church windows . xxx s.

Item, to Richard Hall, for his yeres wages . . . v s. iiij d.

Item, for lightes to the church, as well torches, white
candles, and waxe . . . . v s. j d. ob.

Item, for a newe booke appointed to be bought by the
busshoppe, made ageinst rebellion [1] . . . xij d.

Item, paid for sundrie worckes and reparacons done by
the seid churchwardens, as appereth by theier booke
of accompt at this tyme delivered . . vij li. v s. ij d.

Some paid xiij li. vj s. vij d. ob.

Recept' eodem anno.

The pascall and tokens money . . . . xxxviij s. iiij d.

Item, for the quarter money of the churche . vj li. xiij s. iiij d.

---

[1] Of course this entry relates to the rebellion in the North in 1569-70.

Item, unto Walter Langford, one pewe next unto the
churche weddinge docre, belonginge heretofore unto
his aunte dame Ales Rogers, received for the same
to the use of the church . . . . .   iiij s.

Item, one pewe graunted to m^r Edmunde Walter by
the bailiffes, belonginge heretofore to Robert Mullynour, lately decessed, beinge on the middle rowe
of pewes on the southe syde by the pyller downe-
ward, next unto the clocke . . . .   v s.

Item, the seid m^r Walter did exchaunge the seid pewe
with Anne Mullynour for another pewe, lyenge
foure pewes upward on that rowe, by assent of
the bailiffes.

Item, the seid m^r Walter did exchaunge the seid pewe
had of Anne Mullynour with William Partrich and
William Bowdlour, by thassentes of the seid bayliffes.

Item, to Robert Lewes, the further halfe of one pewe
lyeng in the midle rowe of pewes on the south side
the church, belonginge heretofore unto his wief,
lately decessed, paid for the same . . .   iij s.

Item, graunted unto William Glover, one pewe, beinge
in the middle rowe where the pulpit standeth, being
the lowest pewe of the rowe, by thassent of Anne
Mulliner, widowe . . . . . .   xij d.

Item, received for William Byrington burieng place or
grave, the first daie of Marche . . . . vj s. viij d.

Item, received for the burienge place of John Alsoppe,
the xxiiijth daie of June . . . . . vj s. viij d.

Item, received of Robert Warton, for his burienge place
in the churche, the xiiijth daie of July . . vj s. viij d.

Item, received of Robert Mullynour, for his burienge
place in the church, the xvijth daie of Auguste . vj s. viij d.

Item, received of Johane Lewys, the xvth day of Sep-
tembre, for her burieng place in the church . vj s. viij d.

Item, received of sir John Symkes, clerke, by the handes
of Richard Cupper, geven to the churche . . iij s. iiij d.

Item, received of John Passic, by an order taken heretofore by m^r justice Throckmorton, to be paid
yerely . . . . vj s. viij d.

Item, m^r Edward Foxe, gent. gave unto the church
one longe lader as apperteygning.

Item, Richard Stanwey of Stanley, lately decessed, by
his will gave to the church one dyaper tableclothe.

Item, received for an old rope, beinge worne and broken
in sundry places . . . . . xij d.

Item, received of Walter Taylour . . . viij s.

        Summa recept' . . xj li. xvj s.

And so remayninge to the churchewardens to be paid to
theim . . .   . . . xxx s. vij d. ob.

The accompt of Kydd ap Edward and Richard Cupper, churchewardens of the towne of Ludlowe, elect in the feast of Symon and Jude, in anno regni regine Elizabethe, etc. xij°., anno Domini 1570, for one holle yere then next ensuing, and then bailieffes William Poughnell and Moris Philipes elect, and at the hearing of this accompt bailieffes elect Robert Mason and Richard Hoock, 1571.

In primis, to the decon for his waigees . . . iiij li.

Item, paied to the decon for the keping of the chymes vj s. viij d.

Item, paied to Thomas Season, for his yeres waigees xx s.

Item, paied to Richard Halle, for his yeres waigees in
making cleane the churche . . . . vj s. iiij d.

Item, paied to Crockett for his yeres waigees . iiij s.

Item, paied to the last churchwardens, by the appointcement of m^r bailieffes, for arreragees .   .   .   xxx s.

Item, for lightes to the church, as well torches as waxe candles and tallowe .   ·   .   .   .   iij s. v d. ob.

Item, a sirplesse for Cressett .   ·   .   .   .   iiij s. vij d.

Item, paied for sundry worckes and reparacions don by the churchewardens, as appereth by theire booke at this tyme delyvered .   .   .   .   .   xiij li. vj s.

Summa totalis paied, xx li. xvj s. iiij d.

Recept' eodem anno.

The paschalle and token money .   .   .   .   xliij s.

The quartrege money .   .   .   .   vij li. xiiij d.

Item, received for Robert Lewis buriall .   .   .   vj s. viij d.

Item, received for m^r Pope his buriall .   .   vj s. viij d.

Item, received for Thomas Fraunck .   .   vj s. viij d.

Item, received for Richard Swansons wief .   .   vj s. viij d.

Item, received for m^r Badger his wief .   .   vj s. viij d.

Item, received for Richard Rogers buriall .   .   vj s. viij d.

Item, received for m^{rs} Mydletons buriall .   .   .   vj s. viij d.

Item, received for Robert Stringers buriall .   .   .   v s. viij d.

Item, received for Stringes wiefes buriall .   .   .   vj s. viij d.

Item, received for John Clees wiefes buriall .   .   vj s. viij d.

Item, received for m^{rs} Dedicotes buriall .   .   vj s. viij d.

Item, received for William Lanes buriall .   .   .   vj s. viij d.

Summa .   xiij li. iiij s. ij d.

The receiptes for pewes letten this yere as followeth.

Whereas Robert Stringer, deceased, had one haulf pewe for a kneling place for his wief, also deceased, in the pewe with Hughe ap Jevun, on the north side of the church ; The wardens of the church for this yere, by thassent of the bailieffes of the towne,

have graunted the saide haulf pewe to James Fe-
nell, goldsmith, to have and enjoye the same in as
ample manner as the said Stringer had the same;
provided never the lesse, if the said James do de-
parte owt of this towne to dwell in another place,
and be absent one holle yere together, his interest
in the said pewe to determyne. And it shalbe
lawfull to the bailieffes and churchwardens then
being to graunt the same over to another person,
for the benifite of the parish. And it [is] agreed and
graunted that the said James shall paye to the use
of the reparacons of the church, to thandes of the
said wardens, the somme of vj s. for the said haulf
pewe. Provided also that he shall not by any
meanes advaunce the said pewe to any higher alti-
tude, or streitch it owt in leingth or breadthe, then
it nowe is, upon payne of forfeiture [of] his interest.
The residowe of all the pewes hereafter to be
graunted with like fforme   .   .   .   .   .   vj s.

Item, received of Charles Bouth and Roger Brodshowe,
   gent., for a pewe late Robert Stringers, decessed,
   at our Lady chauncell dore, on the south side the
   church, the some of .   .   .   . xiij s. iiij d.
And in like forme above written.

Item, received of Elizabeth Rogers, widowe, for one
   haulf pewe in the south midle rowe in the church,
   late Robert Lewes, deceased, the some of   .   .   v s.
And in like forme.

Item, received of John Butt, for haulf a pewe with
   Humffrey Hynton, late surrendred by John So-
   therne to the parish use, on the north ile of the
   church   .   .   .   .   ij s.
And in like covenauntes.

And whereas Thomas Blashfield hathe haulf a pewe
where m^{rs} Alsopp kneleth, in the north mydle ile,
he hath surrendred the same and his interest therin,
and thereupon the same ys graunted to William
Browne, for the some of v s., with v s. in consideracon of the late service don by the said Browne in
the tyme of his being churchwarden, and in consideracon also of the yelding up of another pece of
grownde, appoincted him to make a pewe upon, ys
qualified unto xij d., and he to enjoye the same
upon the like covenantes   .   .   .   .   .   xij d.

Item, received of m^r Ellice ap Ellice, gent. for one pewe,
late of Elinour Dedicote, widowe, deceased, on the
northe ile of the church, nere unto St. Johns
chauncell dore, the some of   .   .   x s.

And under thother covenauntes.

Item, received of William Chelmick the yonger, for
one haulf pewe on the south ile, late John Gruffithes thelder, decesed, with John Merston   .   iiij s.

And under like covenauntes.

Item, received of John Bent and John Davies, cordiner,
for one pewe surrendred unto the parish by Walter
Bouldes wief, in the lower end of the north ile   .   ij s.

And under like covenauntes before.

Item, received of William Harries, for one pewe, surrendred by Richard Baugham to the parish use,
beneath the north dore   .   .   .   .   •   iiij s.

By like covenauntes.

Item, Kydd ap Edward and Richard Cupper, church
wardens, one haulf pewe with John Shepert, on the
south ile, late William Eatons, deceased, for the
somme of   .   .   .   .   xij d.

In consideracon of theire service this yere.

Item, received of Lawrence Beck, for haulf a pewe in the north ile, late Lewes Philipes, deceased, and receaved for the same   .   .   .   .   ij s.

    Received for the pewes. Summa l s. iiij d.

    Summa totalis oneris paied xx li. xvj s. iiij d.

    Summa totius rec' xiij li. iiij s. ij d.

And so the church oweth to the churchewardens upon this accompte   .   .   .   .   . v li. xxij d.

    Receaved for the pewes   .   .   l s. iiij d.

The accompt of Thomas Canlande and Richard Brasier, churchewardens of the towne of Ludlowe, elect in the feaste of Simon and Jude, in anno regni regine Elizabethe, etc. xv°., anno Domini 1571, for one holle yere then next ensuinge, and then bayelieffes Robert Mason and Richard Hooke elect, and at the hearinge of this accompt Lawrence Bake and John Brasier, 1572.

Inprimis, payd to Edward Darbye, for fower horsses and him selfe to go to Bewedley for lyme, to make an end of whittinge the churche   .   .   .   vij s.

Payd the same lyme at Bewedlye, beinge x[th] boshelles .   v s.

Payd for wyer to mend one of the chimes   .   ·   .   ij d.

Payd to Richardes for that was unpayd to him for whittinge of the churche   .   .   .   .   .   x s

Payd for xvj li. of rede lede for the redinge of the churche   .   .   .   .

Payd Richardes for the redinge of the churche   .   xl s.

Payd for j li. of candelles   .   .   .   .   iiij d. ob.

Payd for yevie and hollye agaynste Christmas   .   vj d.

Payd for iij li. of candelles agaynste Christmas   .   x d. ob.

Payd to Thomas Higges, his quarters wages, dew at Christmas laste   .   .   .   .   .   xxvj s. viij d.

Payd for a lynke to servise at the communion on Christmas daie . . . .   viij d.

Payd to a straunger, for mendinge the clocke at m^r
baylyeffes apoyntment . . . . . ij s. viij d.

Payd for browne colors for to color the porche . .   vj d.

Payd for naylles to mende two of the belle whilles on
Twellfe evin . . . . . . ·   iij d.

Payd for mendinge the longe sceate before the pulpitte   ij d.

Payd for ij li. of candelles for Higges . . .   vij d.

Payd for makinge a keye and for mendinge the loke of
the chest in the vestree . . . .   iij d.

Payd for makinge clene saynt Johns chansell .   iiij d.

Payd Thomas Season his quarters wagis, dwe at Christmas . . . .   v s.

Payd for naylles to mende the lokers of the belles .   j d.

Payd ij li. of candelles the iij. daie of Januarie . .   vij d.

Paid John Roo, for mendinge the bere, and makinge
newe lokers, and wod to make them, and mendinge
one bell wheell . . . . iij s. ij d.

Paid for j li. of syes candle . . . . .   xv d.

Payd for makin clene saynt Margettes chancell .   iiij d.

Paid for mendinge the glase lantorne . .   ij d.

Paid for ij li. of candelles . . . . . .   vj d.

Paid to Richard Swanson for a roope to peace on of the
belle roopes . . . . ij s. ij d.

Paid for cordes to drawe the organes at severall tymes   iij d.

Paid Thomas Season for his quarters wayges, dwe at
Easter . . . .   v s.

Paid Thomas Higges his quarters wages, dwe at the
same time . . . . xxvj s. viij d.

Paid for a corde for the morninge prayer bell . .   x d.

Paid m^r Farres man Coxshall for raittes heades, at the
apoyntment of m^r baylyeff Mason .   xij d.

Paid master chancelers man for regestringe the xij. mens
names of the visitacion at Easter, and readinge over
the articles . . . . xij d.

Paid master Pinners charges and Thomas Canlandes, in
ridinge to Tenburye to deliver our presentment xij d.

Paid for hache [1] nayles to mend one of the bell whelles
in Aprill . . . . ij d.

Paid for makinge a newe stoke to the second tenor . vij s.

Paid for newe brasinge the fore bell . . . . viij d.

Paid to Gethinge, for iij[th] daies worke to mend the
whelles of the belles, and mendinge the stoke of the
second tenor, and brasinge her . . . . ij s. iij d.

Paid for mendinge the second bell whell and brasinge
her . . . . xx d.

Paid for a xj[th] loodes of xij[th]. fote longe to laye in the
steple sollars . . . . vij s. iiij d.

Paid for nayles to the bell whelles . . . . j d.

Paid for a boshell of and halfe of slaked lyme to mend
the walles and chinckes of the sough ile . . iiij d.

Payd for mos to put betwene the ledes of the churche ⸪ iiij d.

Paid for a boshell of charkcolles for the mendinge of
the leades . . . . iiij d.

Paid for a peace of tember to pute under the leade of the
south ile . . . . x d.

Paid for a keye for the skolars chancell doore . . iij d.

Paid for ij c. and xxj li. of leade to the churche at a j d.
the li. . . . . xx s. v d.

Paid Season his quarters wages, dwe at Mydsomer laste v s.

Paid for vj. hoppes [2] of charkcoll for the plimar mor [3] . vj d.

Paid for ij[th] horse loode of lyme to point the wales upon
the leades . . . . x d.

---

[1] This word has not occurred before.

[2] A hoop, a measure said to contain about four pecks.

[3] For the plumber more, i.e. in addition to what he had been previously supplied with.

Paid for nayles to the lead on the roffe of the churche   ij d.

Paid Thomas Higges his quarters wages, dwe at Mid-
somer   .   .   .   .   xxvj s. viij d.

Paid for colles more   .   .   .   .   .   .   iij d.

Paid Corbet his yeres wages   .   .   .   iiij s.

Paid for rossen for the plemer[1] .   .   .   .   ij d.

Paid j li. of candles, the xjth of October   .   iij d. ob.

Paid for lyme more   .   .   .   .   .   .   iij d.

Paid for a dandrick[2] for the second tenor   .   .   ij s.

Paid for mendinge another baudricke   .   .   .   iiij d.

Paid for j. li. candelles more   .   .   .   .   iij d. ob.

Paid Thomas Higges his quarters waiges, dwe at Myg-
hallmas   .   .   .   .   xxv s. viij d.

Paid Thomas Season his quarters waiges, dwe the
same tyme .   .   .   .   v s.

Paid for ringe and a staple and settinge him in at the
arche of the pulpitte .   .   .   .   .   .   iiij d.

Paid for xiiij. li. of sother, occupied on the leades a vj li.   vij s.

Paid William Burges, for xiij. daies worke on the leades,
a x d. the daie .   .   .   .   x s. x d.

Payd for makinge clene the leades and gutters at divers
tymes   .   .   .   .   xij d.

Paid for makinge clene master baylyef scate, iiij d., and
for two burden of roshes to strawe it agayne   .   viij d.

Paid Burges for makinge bigger the same pewe doore,
and for his tymber and nayles   .   .   .   ij s. viij d.

Paid Higges for kepinge the chymes   .   .   vj s viij d.

Paid for iij li. of candelles   .   .   .   x d. ob.

Paid for j. li. of syes candles   .   .   .   .   x d.

Paid for a bare to the churche grates and puttinge yt in   vj d.

Paid to Richard Halle his holl yeres waiges   .   v s. iijd.

---

[1] The plumber.

[2] This is distinctly written in the original, but perhaps it is an error for *baudrick*, espe-
cially as " another " baudricke is spoken of in the next line.

Paid to the ringares, the xvij[th] of this November, that
    range for the quene,[1] at the appoyntment of m[r]
    baylieffes, in money and drincke .   .   .   .   x s.
Paid to Steven Knight, for makinge xxxiiij[th] great
    nayles for the brasinge of iij[th] belles, and a classpe
    to on whelle   .   .   .   .   xij d.
Paid him for ij[th] staples   .   .   .   .   .   iiij d.
Paid for a boele to the baudricke of the second tenor   ij d.
Paid for makinge newe the gogines [2] of the second tenor
    when the stoke was newe mad, and for makinge
    faste the hoppes [3]   .   .   .   .   .   viij d.
Paid for cuttinge of the claper of the second tenor   .   iiij d.
          Somma   .   .   xv li. xviij s. vij d.
Receaved as herafter followeth and appereth   .   .xiij li. v s. vj d.
Receaved of m[r] Richard Hucke for the surrender of a
    pewe from mastres Hanley, as appereth in our re-
    ceyttes on the other syde   .   .   .   .   .   xij d.
Receaved more, as appereth in our receattes   .   .   xvj s. iiij d.
        So rested dwe to us juste xxxv s. ix d.
More paid to sir Richard, for kepinge the boke of
    buringe and christeninge   .   .   .   .   .   ij s.
        So rested dwe to us xxxvij s. ix d.

Receates receaved by us the said churchewardence in
this forsaid yere of our beinge in office as followethe.

Inprimis receaved of the parishenars for the token
    money at Easter   .   .   .   .   .   xlij s.
Receaved of Richardes for lime that was spare of whit·
    inge the churche   .   .   .   .   .   v s.
Receaved for broken peaces of leade that wee had spare,
    beinge delivered d. c. at a j d. the pounde   .   .   iiij s. viij d.

---

[1] This was the day of Queen Elizabeth's accession to the throne.
[2] The gudgeons, or pins on which the wheels of the bells worked.   [3] Hoops.

Receave for pewes that wee have graunted this yere as
followeth, unto the parties whose names are under
written.

Of William Allsope, for hallfe a pewe with William
Browne, late beinge his mothers, in the north yle
afore the pulpite . . . . . . x s.

Of master Rascoll, for hallfe a pewe, late master Drapers,
lyinge in, the lower end of the churche, on the
north side . . . . iij s. iiij d.

Of master Fare and master John Taylor, for the makinge
perfect of their recorde for on pewe afore the pulpite, surrendred to them by William Challmicke
thelder deceasyd, in the tyme of William Browne
and Thomas Shrawley, churche wardens . . iiij s.

And allso for on pewe in the lower end of the churche,
that master Farr assigned to the said William Chel-
micke, in the yere above saide, it is nowe agreed
that the same pewe do nowe comme into the handes
of master Fare agayne.

Of Thomas Canland, for hallfe a pewe in the mydle
northe yle, with master Richard Hucke, late mr
John Coxe, deceased . . . . . ij s.

Of Richard Brasier, for hallfe a pewe on the north syde
the churche, with John Clee, surrendered into the
parishes handes by master bayliefe Brasier, late
his wyffes . . . . xij d.

Of William Reynolles, walker, for hallfe a pewe with
Edward Doughtie, on the south syd the churche
above the dore, whiche he helde by his late wyffe iij s. iiij d.

Receave for buryalles in the churche as followeth, this
yere as followethe.

Receave for the buringe of the ollde Langham . . vj s. viij d.

Receave for the buriall of John Bubbe . . vj s. viij d.

Receave for the buriall of one Charlles Powell, a
    straunger . . . . vj s. viij d.
Receave for the buriell of mystres Allsope . . . vj s. viij d.
Receave for the buriell of mᵣ Ellice Evans, gent. . vj s. viij d.
Receave for the buriall of mᵣ Richard Blashfildes wyfe . vj s. viij d.
Receave for the buriall of John Thomkyes . . vj s. viij d.
Receave of Hughe ap Jevun for the buriall of his
    wyfe . . . . vj s. viij d.
Receave for the buriall of mᵣ John Coxe ·   ·   . vj s. viij d.
Receave of the parishnares the money for the hole yere,
    as dothe appere by our booke . . . vj li. x s. ij d.
        Somme of receyttes is xiij li. v s. vj d.
Receave more of master Richard Hucke, for one littell
    pewe, beinge one the southe syde of the churche,
    beneath the doore, surrendered into the perishe
    handes by mastres Hanley . . . . . xij d.
Receave more of the parishnars for their quarteradge
    money . . . . xvj s. iiij d.
        Somma totallis to our receyttes xiiij li. ij s. x d.

VILLA DE
LUDLOWE.
  The accomptes of Roger Clerke and Hughe
ap Jevan, churchewardens of the saied
towne, from the feaste of Simon and
Jude, anno Domini 1572, untill thende
of one yeare then next ensuynge, in the
tyme of Laurence Beck and John Brasier then bailiffes of the saiede towne,
1573.

Inprimis, paiede for diverse expences and for a pauper
    booke,[1] as appereth by bille . . . ij s. iiij d.

---

[1] A paper book, probably.

Item, for mendinge the belles, belle ropes, and thorgans.
as appereth by bille . . . . . xvj s. x d.
Item, for workmanshipp donn upon the churche at sun-
dric tymes, as appereth by bille. . . . xxj s. ij d.
Item, for candles, as welle waxe as tallowe, to thuse of
the churche, as apperethe by bille . . . vj s. iij d.
Item, for ringinge at sundrie tyms, as appereth by bille   ix s. iiij d.
Item, for makinge a newe sherples, a new ladder, and
for leade to the churche, as apperethe by bille . iiij s. j d.
Item, paiede to the deacon for his wages and settinge the
chymes, to Thomas Season, Richarde Halle, and
Crockett, for there wages, and to the curatt for
keapinge the booke of christenynge. . vij li. iiij s. viij d.
Suma totius alloc. est x li. iij s. viij d.

The Receiptes for pewes as followeth.

Inprimis, reccavede at Easter of token money . . xlv s. x d.
Item, for the burialle of mistres Passie . . . vj s. viij d.
Item, for the burialle of ser William Badger . . vj s. viij d.
Item, for the burialle of William Harries . . . vj s. viij d.
Item, of James Fennelle for a peace of grounde in the
Ladies chauncelle to make a pewe . . . xx d.
Item, of Robert Bubbe and William Mason for the iiij[th]
pewe in the same chauncelle, beinge to them by us
sett . . . . vj s. viij d.
Item, of Richarde Blashfielde for half a pewe with m[r]
Season lyinge in the southe ile of the churche . xij d.
Item, of Andrewe Sonnybanke and William Boliler,
walker,[1] for a pewe in the southe ile of the churche
surrendred by m[r] Partriche . . . . iiij s.
Item, of m[r] Beck for half a pewe in the upper end of
the south ile of the churche with m[res] Ellis, which
late was m[r] Barnabies . . . . . v s.

_____

A walker was what we now call a fuller.

Item, of Thomas Candlande and Edwarde Crowther for
a pewe lyinge in the northe ile of the churche
anontes[1] St. Margarettes chauncelle, surrendrede
by master Becke . . . . xij d.
Item, of Walter Tailor for the Breake Closse . . viij s.
Item, for quartridge money . . . . vij li. iiij s. ix d.
    Suma totius oneris . . xj li. xvij s. xj d.
So the churchwardens owe on theire allowance   xxxiiij s. iij d.
    Which they have paiede and are therof discharged.

VILLA DE   The accompte of Richarde Grove and John
LUDLOW.   Dalton, churchwardens of the saide
            towne, from the feaste of Simon and
            Jude, anno Domini 1573, untill the
            ende of one holle yere then next ensu-
            ynge, in the tyme of John Belle and
            William Powes, then bailiffes of the
            saiede towne, 1574.

Money receavede by the saide churchwardens as followeth.

Inprimis at Easter for paschall and token money   . lvj s.
Item, for quartrige money . . . . vij li. ij s. iij d.
Item, of master Saye for his grave in the churche   vj s. viij d.
Item, for the grave of Thomas Wheller, gent. . . vj s. viij d.
Item, recevede of Richarde Hopton for halff a pew late
    Richarde Stanweis, deceassed, on the south side of
    the churche, with William Bradshaw thelder   . vj s.
Item, Symon Thornton, scholemaster, for a pew nere
    master bailiffes pew, surrendrede by Richarde
    Dier . . . . xij d.

[1] Opposite.

Item, of John Rawlinges, husbande, for half a pewe
   under the deske by the pulpitt, surrendrede by
   Simon Thornton   .   .   .   .   .   .   ij s. vj d.

Item, of Thomas Bedow, milner, for a pewe late Anne
   Addames, his mother in lawe decessede, anonte the
   fonte on the further side   .   .   .   .   .   v s.

Item, of Robert Bubbe for half a pew, surrendrede by
   his mother, in the southe side of the churche   .   xx d.

Item, of John Bell thelder, now bailiffe, for a pece of
   grownde nere the Ladies chauncelle dore, for to
   make a pew uppon   .   .   .   .   .   ij s.

Item, of Richarde Grove, for another peace of grounde,
   next beneath hym   .   .   .   .   .   ij s.

Item, of Walter Dedicott, for another peace of grounde,
   next beneathe the same pewe   .   .   .   .   ij s.

Item, of Richarde Philipes, capper, for the fourthe pewe
   in the Ladie chauncelle   .   .   .   .   .   iij s. iiij d.

Item, of John Belle thelder and Richard Grove, for
   theire pewe dores and the hinges of the same   .   iij s.

Item, due of master Passie for Portmans medowe, accord-
   inge to an order therin taken by master justice [and
   by hym unpaied, vj s. viij d.] [1]
         Summa totalis rec. est xij li. j d.

Disbursede by the saiede churchwardens as followeth.

Inprimis, for drinck at the laste accompt daie   .   .   ij s. iiij d.

Item, paied Thomas Higges for ringinge daie bell at
   Easter.   .   .   .   .   ij s.

Item, paied him for ringinge the xvij[th] daie of November, beinge the firste daie of the quenes majesties
   raigne   .   .   .   .   vj s.

Item, paied for makinge cleane the steple   .   .   .   viij d.

Item, more for makinge clene the steple of snowe   .   iiij d.

[1] The words within brackets are crossed out in the original.

Item, paied to Thomas Season for his yeares wages for mendinge the glasse wyndowes . . . . xx s.

Item, paied him for mendinge the glasse in sainct Johns chauncell, beinge broken by a lunatick . . vij s.

Item, paied him for mendinge the leades over the churche xij d.

Item, paied to Richard Halle for his yeres wages for keapinge clene the churche . . . . v s. iiij d.

Item, paiede to John Crockett for his yeres wages to kepe the dogges oute of the churche . . . iiij s.

Item, paide to Richard Halle for hollies to dresse the churche . . . . vj d.

Item, paiede for a bell roppe . . . . . v s. vj d.

Item, for nayles and leather . . . . . iij d.

Item, to Burges for shootinge the belle roppes . . x d.

Item, for nayles to fasten the belle wheale . . . iij d.

Item, to Burges for brasinge upon a belle . . . xij d.

Item, for twoe lynckes at Christmas . . . . xvj d.

Item, geaven to ryngers in Christmas to drinck . vj d.

Item, for a ladder . . . . iij s. viij d.

Item, to John for makinge a key and settinge on hinges vj d.

Item, for a lock to hange uppon the cheste . . . vij d.

Item, for a purse . . . . j d.

Item, for nayles and leather for the lockettes . . iiij d.

Item, for a paper booke . . . . . . iiij d.

Item, for ringinge daie belle when the judges where here at the request of master bailiffes . · . xij d.

Item, for lyme and sande to pave the Ladie chauncelle xij d.

Item, for Earles wages . . . . . ij s.

Item, to Stephen Knighte for iij^e hokes to hange the ladder · · · . . . . . xviij d.

Item, for nailes and leather to the beare [1] . . . iiij d.

Item, to Higges, for ringinge daie belle at master bailiffes appointment . . . . . . xij d.

[1] The bier.

Item, to William Wale, for a baldricke for one of the
    clapers of the belles .   .   .   .   .   x d.

Item, to Stephen Knighte, for makinge a buckle and a
    plate for the beare, and for mendinge the hinges
    of the church dore .   .   .   .   .   xd.

Item, to Richarde Swanson, for iron to mende the
    chymes .   .   .   .   ix d.

Item, for shotinge of ij^c ropes and coles and daies wages   xx d.

Item, for nayles .   .   .   .   .   .   v d.

Item, more to Burges for mendinge the belle whele   }
Item, for his laber and nayles .   .   .   } viij d.

Item, to master Farr, the 20. of June, for lynnen
    clothe to make ij°. surpleses for Higges sonnes,[1]
    and for makinge the same .   .   .   .   v s.

Item, paiede at my goinge to Hereford .   .   ij s. viij d.

Item, for swepinge the windowes and pavinge in the
    chauncelle and in the churche .   .   .   xiiij d.

Item, paiede at Michaelmas for one li. of waxe .   .   x d.

Item, to Higges for swepinge of the churche.

Item, for shotinge of ij^c. ropes .   ·   .   .   iiij d.

Item, for a peace of tymber to make a sylle and one
    grate of tymber at the challence next the col-
    ledge .   .   .   .   x d.

Item, for a new post and a key to the southe challence[2]   x d.

Item, for nailes .   .   .   .   .   .   iij d.

Item, to Roe and his man .   .   .   .   .   xvj d.

Item, for twoe boordes to bere the water from Franckes
    house .   .   .   .   xij d.

Item, to Dyke the tiler for one daies worck, the 9. of
    October, for mendinge the challence .   .   .   ix d.

---

[1] The surplices so often mentioned in these accounts were for the choristers, and some probably for the scholars of the Grammar School.

[2] This was no doubt the liche-gate by which the churchyard was entered from Broad Street, on the site of what is still called the Callends.

Item, for a runge [1] of lyme . . . . . v d.
Item, for tilestones . . . . iiij d.
Item, for a rope for the organs . . . . . ij d.
Item, to John Roe for mendinge the churche doore . viij d.
Item, for nayles at the same tyme . . . . iiij d.
Item, for a plancke to mende the same . . . vj d.
Item, paiede to James the somner for the parishe . iiij d.
Item, to Thomas Higges, for a pounde and a quarter of
scisses and a pounde of kandles . . . . xx d.
Item, for mendinge the Psalter and the register booke xij d.
Item, for makinge cleane the steple and the leades . vij d.
Item, paiede to the commissionar for takinge the pre-
sentement of the register booke . . . . xij d.
Item, paiede for wyne and sugar at the newe house to
m^r bailiffes and the comissionar . . . . iij s.
Item, paiede to Gruffith the smythe, for makinge a key
for the boxe . . . . iiij d.
Item, paiede to William Burges for mendinge iij^e
belles . . . . xij d.
Item, paiede to the archedeacons man for writinge oure
veredict . . . . vj d.
Item, to Thomas Acrew for a new baldrick to the third
belle . . . . xij d.
Item, to Edwarde Humfreis for lymynge over the ves-
trye . . . . iiij d.
Item, paiede to Thomas Higges for mendinge iij^e bell-
ropes . . . . vj d.
Item, for xx^ti pounde of candles . . . . . v s.
Item, paiede to Higges for his holle yeres wages v li. vj s. viij d.
Item, paiede to him for keapinge the chymes . . vj s. viij d.
Item, paiede to sir Robert Wilcokes for keapinge the
churche booke of weddinge, christenynge, and
buryinge . . . . ij s.

---

[1] A name of a measure which seems to be forgotten.

Item, for other charges . . . . . .   viij d.
Item, allowed them more for further expences   ·   .   ij s.
   Summa totalis paiede . . xj li. vj s.
    So the churchewardens owe over theire
     allowances . . x s. j d.
  Whiche they have paiede, and are therof dischargede.

APPENDIX.

I. Extracts from the Churchwardens' Accounts from 1575 to 1600.

1574 to 1575, Robert Wright and . . . . . . churchwardens.

Item, at Didleburie for the dynner of thenquest at the
visitacon . . . . ix s.

Item, for oure horse meate there . . . . . iiij d.

Item, to the register for the coppie of the booke of articles xij d.

Item, more to him for entringe oure names . . . xij d.

Item, paiede at Cleberie for oure dinner when we deli-
verede up oure presentment to the bushoppe . . ij s. viij d.

Item, for oure horse meate there . . . . xi d.

*   *   *   *

Item, for searchinge the foundacon of the churche, to
Jorden, for ij^e daies, and to Higges, Humfreis, and
Careles, the same tyme for the like . . . iij s. iiij d.

*   *   *   *

Item, for washinge the table clothes of the churche at
sundrye tymes . . . . vj d.

*   *   *   *

Mr Passie oweth this yere for Portman medowe, according to the order taken by m^r justice, vj s. viij d.

Also Walter Taylor oughte this yere to paie for the
Breke closse . . viij d.

1576 to 1577, Richard Hopton and William Walle, churchwardens.

Inprimis, paied for a drinckinge, the 4. of December,
1576, at the goinge oute of the olde churchwardens,
by m^r bailiffes appointement . . . . ij s.

Item, paied Humfreis for pullinge downe an aultar stone
   in the churche, and for trymynge the place where it
   stodd . . . .   xvj d.

*   *   *   *

Item, for mendinge the poore mans boxe . . .   viij d.
Item, for excusinge oure apperaunce at Stretton before
   the comissaries . . . .   ij s.

*   *   *   *

Item, the 9. of January, spent at Tenbury for our dynner   xij d.
Item, for horsemeate the same tyme . . . .   ix d.

*   *   *   *

Item, to Humfreis for dabinge the churche house .   vj d.
Item, for a lock for the same house . . . .   vj d.

*   *   *   *

Item, spent at Leyntwardyn when I went to the comys-
   sary . . . .   ix d.
Item, for courte fees that tyme . . . . .   vj d.
Item, a loade of cley for the churche house . .   iiij d.
Item, paied Giles Bruton, for a rattes heade and a wontes [1]   j d.
Item, for our apperaunce at Stretton, and courte fees   xij d.
Item, for ij^e mattes for the churche . . . .   xvj d.
Item, for a sill for the churche house . . .   ij s.
Item, for caryinge it from the sawpitt to churche   iiij d.
Item, for worckmanship there . . .   iij s. xj d.

*   *   *   *

Item, for lyme to pargitt the churche house . .   vj d.
Item, to Humfreis for worckmanship there . .   vj d.
Item, for keapinge the chauncell doore on Easter daie   ij d.
Item, at the visitacon to the archdeacons man for fees   iiij d.
Item, to Crew for a baldrop and for nailes . .   ij s. ij d.
Item, to m^r Farr for a booke of Erasmus . .   viij s.

*   *   *   *

---

[1] A mole is still called a *wont*, in Shropshire. On the destruction of vermin by Act of Parliament, to which this wont was a victim, see before, the note on p. 139 of the present volume.

Item, for makinge the presentment at the visitacon   vj d.

Item, that daie for wyne and sugar to m^r deane   .   ix d.

Item, to Gyles Bruton for xx^{tie} wontes heades   .   .   x d.

Item, for half a strick of coales   .   .   .   .   ij d.

1577 *to* 1578.   *Thomas Hunte and Gruffithe Nalle, churchwardens.*

Item, paied, the 18 of Marche, for the xij^e mens dynner
     at Mounslowe, at the visitacon, and the makinge a
     booke   .   .   .   .   .   .   vij s. j d.

           *   *   *   *

Item, paied for a pottell of sacke and a pottell of clarett
     geaven to m^r Verion by m^r bailieffes appointment   ij s. vj d.

1578 *to* 1579.   *Edward Crowther and William Beck, churchwardens.*

Item, payd Burges for takinge downe the ij^e pynacles
     of the steple and bringinge of them downe into the
     churche and churchouse   .   .   .   .   xij s. vj d.

           *   *   *   *

Item, to John Cooke, iiij^{or} quiers of pott paper   .   .   xvj d.

1597 to 1580.   *Roger Gruffithes and John Perckes, churchwardens.*

Item, for proces from the counsaille by the comaunde-
     ment of m^r bailiffes againste m^r Passye touchinge
     the ducties of the churche   .   .   .   .   xxij d.

Item, for v^e bookes of prycksonge   .   .   .   ij s.

Item, to Burges for two juystes[1] for the scallyons   .   vj d.

           *   *   *   *

Item, payd at the sittinge of the deane of Dydlebury   .   iiij d.

Item, payd for the receavinge of the verdicte befor the
     chauncellor   .   .   .   .   .   .   viij d.

Item, payd for a horse to goe to Whitborne   .   .   ij s.

Item, payd to the paritory[2]   .   .   .   .   .   vj d.

1580 *to* 1581, *Philip Bradford and John Becke, churchwardens.*

Item, payd for a booke of injunccons for the churche   iiij d.

Item, payd for puttinge the presentment at the buyshops
     visitacon   .   .   .   .   xij d.

---

[1] Joists.   [2] The apparitor.

Item, spent upon the quest of the visitacon . . xij d.

Item, payd for one statute booke at the apoynctment of
mʳ bayliffes . . . . ij s.

    *   *   *   *

Item, payd the sumner for his fee for servinge the sitacon
to Whitbourne . . . . vj d.

Item, puttinge in our presentment at Whitborne . iiij d.

Item, our chardges to Whitborne . . . . ij s. iiij d.

1581 to 1582. *Thomas Bower and Thomas Becke, churchwardens.*

Item, spende in rydinge to Whittborne the 2. of Marche,
and regestringe our names . . . . . ij s. vj d.

Item, payde to William Burges for a stay for thende of
the scallons . . . . iiij d.

   *   *   *   *

Item, payd to Season for takinge downe the glasse and
settinge it up agayne in the weavers chauncell . ij s. x d.

1582 to 1583. *John Crowther and Henry Aumbler, churchwardens.*

Item, payde Cornelyus for turninge and putting up of
xiiijᵉ pillors before the organs . . . . vij s.

Item, payde Parton for tymber to make iiijᵒʳ of them, and
for sawinge of one peece of tymber . . . xvj d.

Item, payd for nayles to fasten the pillors . . . ij d.

Item, payd to Allen for payntinge the said pillors and the
defaced places in the chauncell . . . . iij s. iiij d.

1583 to 1584. *William Bedoe and Robert Saunders, churchwardens.*

Item, for a quiere of paper and glewe for mʳ Harrison . vj d.

Item, payd to Thomas James for the conveyinge of the
certificat for the recusantes . . . . vj d.

Item, payd for iiijᵒʳ Psalmes bookes . . . . iij s. iiij d.

Item, for wyne and bread the vjᵗʰ of Auguste . . v d. ob.

Item, for a pottle of wyne sente to the chauncelour . x d.

Item, payd for the questes dynner at my lo. visitacon vij s. viij d.

Item, payd to Roger Kente for the delyverie of the pre-
sentmentes . . . . vij d.
Item, for a coram nomina . . . . . . iiij s.
Item, for a pynte of goose liker, to liker the belles . iij d.

1584 *to* 1585. *Thomas ap Robert and Thomas Evans, churchwardens.*

Item, paied to a mason for hanginge up the new buck-
ettes on the walle in the churche . . . ij s. vj d.
Item, for ij^e boordes to sett over the callenge for my lorde x d.

1585 *to* 1586. *John Bradforde and Charles Wigley, churchwardens.*

Item, the xth of December, rydinge to Witstanstow, my
fellow and I, and m^r Thomas Evans, for our dyn-
ners and horsemeate . . . . . . ij s.
Item, for ministringe the articles and puttinge in of the
same . . . . ij s.

* * * *

Item, a deske boorde at my lordes seate . viij d.

1586 *to* 1587. *William Bowldler and Thomas Yearothe,*
churchwardens.

Item, payd to Woodward for mendinge the scalen over
agaynst the colledge with a rope . . . . vj d.
Item, paied to Burges for mendinge the churche scalleus iiij d.

* * * *

Item, paied by my fellowe for a quarte of sacke to the
church deacon . . . . . . xij d.
Item, a quier of paper . . . . . . iiij d.
Item, paied to Richard Higges for stoppinge choughes
out of the churche . . . . . . iiij d.
Item, paied to Thomas Clerke, for his workmanshipp
and fyndinge stuffe to doe it aboutes the church
scallens and woorke . . . . . . iij s. iiij d.

1587 to 1588. *Edward Powes and William Gwillim, churchwardens.*

1588 to 1589. *Richard Baldwyn and Richard Benson, churchwardens.*

Item, for the table of consanguinitie, and for a frame to
it . . . .   vj d.
Item, paied for a coram nomina to the chauncelors
officer . . . .   iiij s.

1589 to 1590. *Richard Langford and Thomas Awbrey, churchwardens.*

Item, for vj^e yardes of dowlas to make Crompe a syrples,
the 23 December . . . . . .   vij s.
Item, to goodwife Knighte for makinge the same .   xiij d.
Item, for mendinge the churche kallendes . . .   xv d.
Item, to Thomas Clerke, for ij^o barrs into the skallendes   viij d.

1590 to 1591. *Saunder Williams and William Cooke, churchwardens.*

1591 to 1592. *Rice Thomas and Thomas Powle, churchwardens.*

1592 to 1593. *Richard Seare (?) and Richard Nightingall, churchwardens.*

1593 to 1594. *William Henghes and Richard Edwardes, churchwardens.*

Item, for ringing a peale for William Norton of London
at m^r bailieffes appoyntment . . . .   vj d.
Item, where m^r bailieffes appoynted Thomas Roe to
kepe doges out of the churche for one yere from the
xxiiijth of February, 1593, for v s. wages, wee have
paid him towardes the same wages . . .   iij s.
Item, for a booke of advertisementes, and a booke of
articles . . . .   viij d.
Item, to the jury of the visitacon in bred and drink as
hath bene accustomed . . . . .   xij d.

1594 to 1595. *William Powes and Richard Wilson, churchwardens.*

1595 *to* 1596. *Andrew Sonibanck and John Blewe, churchwardens.*

1596 *to* 1597. *Symon Cupper and Roger Bebbe, churchwardens.*

Item, for rydding the churche kalendes . . . vj d.
Item, paid to John Voill for ij⁰ barres for the scalliens,
and for amendinge the olde . . . . ij s. vj d.

1597 *to* 1598. *William Gregory and John Deyos, churchwardens.*

Item, to Thomas Beavan, smith, for makeinge of the
frame for the hower-classe¹ . . . . xx d.
Item, to William Glover, for oylinge and coloringe yt ij d.

1599 *to* 1600.² *Charles Amyas and James Greene, churchwardens.*

———————

II. REMARKS ON THE HISTORY OF PEWS AS ILLUSTRATED BY
THE LUDLOW CHURCHWARDENS' ACCOUNTS, WITH EXTRACTS
FROM THE CHURCHWARDENS' ACCOUNTS OF ST. MICHAEL,
CORNHILL, IN LONDON.

The history of pews, which is curious and interesting in more
points than one, has been hitherto very obscure, or rather it has
been made obscure by the circumstance that it has usually been
treated by writers who were only slightly acquainted with the docu-
mentary materials for it. At the Congress of the British Archæological Association at Ludlow in 1867, I laid the manuscript of the
Churchwardens' Accounts of Ludlow, here printed, before the meeting, and I called attention to their extreme importance in throwing
light upon this question. These remarks were embodied in a paper

———————

¹ The hour-glass. This is rather an interesting entry, for the use of the hour-glass in
churches is not to be traced further back than about this time. The frame of the hour-
glass was usually attached to the pulpit, or to the wall close by it, and some good examples are still found remaining in our country churches.

² The accounts for the year 1598 to 1599 appear never to have been entered in the
book, and a leaf of the manuscript is left blank.

which was soon afterwards published in the Journal of the British Archæological Association. I repeat them here with slight alteration.

The early history of pews is, as just remarked, obscure, and the accounts usually given are repeated by one writer from another, and are extremely confused and inaccurate. In Dr. Hook's valuable work the *Church Dictionary* we are told that " Pews, according to modern use and idea, were not known till long after the Reformation. Inclosed pews were not in general use before the middle of the seventeenth century ; they were for a long time confined to the family of the patron." The churchwardens' accounts of the town of Ludlow are quite sufficient to show the inaccuracy of this statement. But I find other isolated proofs of the antiquity of the use of the pew. In the English *Mort d'Arthure* of Sir Thomas Malory, printed by Caxton, Sir Galahad, one of the purest of the heroes, who is destined to be the discoverer of the St. Grael, arrives at the monastery in which King Evelake, the companion of Joseph of Arimathea in his visit to Britain, and who had been condemned to live three hundred years, was residing as a monk. 'And," says the text, " on the morn he heard his masse, and in the monastery he fonde a preeste redy at the aulter. And on the ryght syde he sawe *a pewe* closyd with yron." This, no doubt, was not only a pew, but a closed pew. But we can go considerably further back even than this. The celebrated poem of the *Vision of Piers Ploughman* was no doubt composed about the year 1360, and its different texts, which vary considerably, belong all to a period extending not much beyond the middle of the second half of the fourteenth century. In the text represented by Whitaker's edition (p. 95), Wrath, in his confession, says that he was accustomed " to sit among wives and widows shut up in pews," and adds that this was a fact well known to the parson of the parish—

> " Among wyves and wodewes
> Ich am ywoned sute
> Yparroked *in puwes*,
> The parson him knoweth." [1]

[1] The MS. Cotton. Vespas. B. xvi. which gives the same text as Whitaker, reads *sitte*

The verb *parroken*, derived from the word *parrok*, a park, means in its primary sense, to enpark, or inclose like a park, but it was used more generally in the signification of to inclose, or close up. In another part of the poem, in the text represented by my own edition (p. 312), Paul the Hermit is said to have shut himself up in a hermitage —

> " Paul *primus heremita*
> Had *parroked* hymselve,
> That no man myghte hym se
> For mosse and for leves."

The well-known mediæval dictionary, the *Promptorium Parvulorum*, defines the word, " PARROKKYN, or speryn in streyte place," which is, in another MS. expressed by "closyn in straythly," that is, in a narrow place. Under the other word, we have, in the *Promptorium*—

> " SPERYN, or schettyn. *Claudo.*
> SPERYN, and close withein (closyn in, MS. K). *Includo.*
> SPERYN, and schette wythe lokkys. *Sero, obsero.*"

Nobody will surely deny that these early pews were closed in, and no doubt locked. It is curious, too, to remark, in illustration of the passage of *Piers Ploughman*, how often in the Ludlow churchwardens' accounts the possessors of pews are " wives and widows."

I am inclined to think that the word *pew* itself is not of foreign origin, but that it has been originally a word of popular growth, and it appears not to have been in use as belonging to correct literature until rather a late date. I have in vain sought through all the dictionaries, English and Latin, or English and other languages, till towards the latter part of the sixteenth century; and yet in the fourteenth century, when *Piers Ploughman* was written, and, in 1485, when the *Mort d'Arthure* was printed, it must have been well known. It was evidently an obscure word with our early etymologists, who are represented by Junius and Skinner, and whose explanations are very far from satisfactory. They fancied it to be derived from the Latin *podium*, and this notion appears ever since

and *pues : sute* is, of course, only another form of *sitte*, if it be not a mere error of Whitaker's, who was very incorrect in whatever he did.

to have been accepted as a fact without question or inquiry. But there are two objections to this piece of etymology which appear to me very serious. In the first place, the Latin word *podium* never meant a pew ; in the second place, any one acquainted with mediæval philology knows that the word cannot have come from the Latin into English in this form, except through the Romane dialects, either Norman or French, and there does not appear ever to have existed in them any such word with such a meaning. It is true that worthy old Minshewe derives it in rather an indirect manner, for he says the pew was called *podium*, because it stretches out like a foot, *quod ad pedis modum extentet*, but it is an explanation which appears to me not very clear.

In pure Latin, according to Ainsworth, the word *podium* had two meanings—1, an open gallery, a balcony or building jutting out ; 2 (technical), that part of the theatre near the orchestra. In mediæval Latin, according to Ducange, the word had three meanings, of which the first was a support or prop of any kind, anything on which one leans, as a staff, crutch, or walking-stick ; applied also to the part of the form on which the monks leaned in kneeling to prayer. From a debased form of this word, *appodiamentum*, were derived the French words *appui* and *appuyer*. The second meaning given by Ducange is a balcony, taken, of course, from the pure Latin. The third and only other mediæval meaning of the word was a hill, represented by the French *puy*, still represented in names of mountains, as the Puy-de-Dome in Auvergne, with a variety of dialectic forms, as *pou, pee, pic*, etc. We have thus the Pee de St. Germain en Laye, the Pou de Flamanville in Normandy, and the well-known Pic de Teneriffe. It is here represented by the English *peak*.

Our old etymologists quote derivatives from the Latin word, which they pretend are identical with our English *pew*, but not one of them will bear any examination. As I have said, there is no such word in French. They point to *puye* and *puyde* in Flemish and Dutch : but in the first of these languages the word meant only a support ; and in the Dutch dictionary of Hexam, printed in 1678, I find it defined, "*Puye*, a pue or place elevated in a market, to proclaim or cry anything," which is no doubt an adaptation of the old meaning of a balcony. Another Dutch dictionary explains it as signifying "the front of a house, a place from which proclamations are read." The old etymologists appeal also to the Italian *poggio*, which is no doubt derived from *podium*, but they were quite unacquainted with its true meaning. Florio explains it, "*Poggio*, a hill, a block to get on horseback;" and he gives as a diminutive, "*Poggiuolo*, a hillock, a horseblock, a leaning place."

It seems to me evident, from the reasons I have adduced, that our English word *pew* is not derived from the Latin *podium*, but that it is an old popular English word, the derivation of which, as in so many similar cases, has been long forgotten.

Since the foregoing notes were written, I am enabled, through the kindness of a City friend, A. J. Waterlow, Esq., to add to it a number of extracts relating to pews from a still existing series of early churchwardens' accounts, belonging to the parish of St. Michael, Cornhill, London. These accounts begin with the year 1456, the 35th of the reign of King Henry VI. and are continued without interruption down to the year 1475, the 14th of Edward IV., so that they are much older than the allusion in the *Mort d'Arthure*. There is then a long *lacuna*, and the accounts are deficient until 1548, which was the first year of the reign of Edward VI. I will only remark further, that, like those of Ludlow, they give us very valuable information on the character of the pews,[1] and it is highly inte-

---

[1] There can be no doubt that the use of pews in churches was quite common during the fifteenth century. Just as I am correcting this sheet for the press, I open the " Testamenta Vetusta," and find, at p. 266, a will of William Bruges, the first Garter King of Arms, dated at London, Feb. 26, 1449, by which he leaves, among other things to the church of Stanford, money to complete the fabric,—" that is to be understand, in coveryng with lede, glassyng, and makyng of pleyne desques, and of a pleyn rodelofte, and *in puyng of the seyd chirch*, nourt curiously, but pleynly, and in pavyng the hole chirch," &c. Again, at p. 259 of the same volume, we have the will of John Younge, of Herne, dated May 26, 1458, who also left money " to the fabrick of the church of Herne, viz. to make *seats called puinge*, x. marks, so that the same be done within two years after my decease."

resting to have to compare together two series of accounts from such widely distant parts of the kingdom.

1457.   *The 36th of King Henry VI.*

Item, payd for an henge for Russells wyfes pewe, iiij*d.*

1459.   38*th Hen. VI.*

Item, for amendyng of the garnettes of ij pewes, and for nayl to the same, j*d*½.

Item, for amendynge of ij menes pewes and j womans pew, with j*d.* for naill and candell, vij*d.*

1460.   39*th Hen. VI.*

Item, paid to a carpenter workyng by half a day in emendynge of a pew iiij*d.*

Item, for garnettes iiij*d.* and nayles j*d.* spended in the same pew, v*d.*

Item, to a carpenter by a day floryng a pew, and other necessaries, viij*d.*

1464.   4*th Edw. IV.*

Item, payde to Henry Chad, carpenter, for makyng of pewes, xxiiij*s.*

Item, payd for cariage of the said pewes to and fro, iiij*d.*

Item, payde for sconchons for the saide pewes, iiij*d.*

Item, payde for an enge of a pew, vj*d.*

1466.

Item, for nayle for the pewes, iij*d.*

Item, payde to a carpenter for mending of the pewes and dores, vs. vj*d.*

1467.   7*th Edw. IV.*

Item, payed for wode and cole, and for amendyng of the lede over my lady Stokkers pew, j*d*½.

Item, payed to a smyth for makyng of a lok to maister Stokkers pew, viij*d.*

1468.   8*th Edw. IV.*

Item, for makyng of ij new pewes in the chirche, viij*d.*

Item, for amendyng of the olde pewes in the chirche, x*d.*

1469.

Item, payed for iij rat trappes for the chirche, vj*d.*

Item, paid to the raker for caryng awey of the chirche dust whan the pewes were made clene, viijd.

Item,[1] payed for a pair new garnetts for a pew in the chirche, vjd.

Item,[1] payed for amendyng of a pair of olde garnetts, iijd.

Item,[1] for amendyng of olde pewes in the chirche, iijd.

Item, payed for ij pair garnettes and for amendyng of olde pewes in the chirche, ixd.

1470.

Item, payde for mendyng of the pewes in the chirche, iiijd.

Item, payde amendyng of the puys in the chirche, ijd.

Item, for mendyng of a pewe in the chirche, jd.

1471.

Item, paid for amendyng of pewys in the chyrche, and for S. William Barbors almery, and for makyng of the cros in the chyrche yerde, and for naylls, and for tymbre for the cros, and ffor the carpenters labur, xxd.

1473.

Item, for makyng of mayster Stokkers pew, xs. vijd.

Item, payde to a carpenter for mendyng of the pewes in the chirche, and for mendyng of the crosse in the chirchawe, iiijd.

Item, for sconcheons and a felet for the same pewes, ijd.

Item, for nayles for the same pewes, and for the crosse in the chirchaw, iiijd.

Item, for werkmanship and nayle for ij women pewes, ijs. vjd.

1474.

Item, payde for havyng awey of the cherche dust wan the puys wer mad clene, iiijd.

Item, payde for translatyng of the meyres pue, xs. vjd.

Item, payde for makyng of the puys in oure Lady Chapell, xiijs.

With this the accounts of the fifteenth century conclude; we go on to those beginning with the reign of Edward VI.

---

[1] The three entries beginning with this come together. It may be remarked that *garnetts*, in old English, meant hinges.

1548.

Item, payd to the joyner for takynge downe the shryvyng pew and makyng another pew in the same place, iij*s*.

1549.

Item, for mendyng the fore pewe by mystres Tollows, ij*s*.
Item, for mendyng the henges of mystres Bryggs pewe, ij*d*.

1550.

Item, for new joynts and ij cramps for Mr. Machyns pewe dore and
Mr. Stanfylds mayds dore, viij*d*.
Item, for a dore and hynges to Mr. Hunts madys pewe dore, viij*d*.
Item, for henges and nayles, and for mendyng of Mr. Ryxmans pewe
dore, and Hattons wyves pewe, and the setts allso, xij*d*.
Item, p*d* to Harry Cutler, for mendyng of the setts of iiij pews, before
Mrs. Hunts pewe, and for mendyng of the pulpet, and for boords,
skykyngs, and nayles, to mend y*e* churche alley gate, and for
mendyng of y*e* grate in y*e* churche yarde, v*s*. vj*d*.

1551—1552.

Item, for nayles and sprygs to the setting up of the new pewe, vj*d*.
Item, for a skounsyn and a ledge, j*d*.
Item, for raysing of the benche in the foore pewe, and nayles and skon-
syons, ij*d*.
Item, p*d* to y*e* goodman Cutlar for mendyng iij pewes, iiij*d*.
Item, to Garrad Symonds, joynor, for y*e* ij newe pewes which were made
at the dore with yere worke to the same, xlv*s*.
P*d* for a q*r* of borde for the pewes, xij*d*.
P*d* to a joynor for settyng up of a pewe and for tymber, iiij*s*.

1553—1554.

Item, paide for takinge downe the newe pwees that stoode in the chauncell, the bakes towarde the awlter, j*s*. ij*d*.

1554 to 1555.

Gathered in the churche for the pewes for the hole yere, v*li*. v*s*. iiij*d*.
Paide and geven unto Roberte Dickenson in Harpe Alie when his wyfe
was brought to bed of ij children, by the consente of some of the
masters of the parish, v*s*.

1555 to 1556.

Paide for wrytinge on the pewe dores at my lorde of Londons commandemente, xij*d*.

1563. *Orders at a vestry meeting on the 16th of May.*

Order for keping their pewes on pain to forfeit ij*d*. the first tyme, and iiij*d*. the second.

Item, ony man that on the hollie day kepeth not his owne pewe, but setteth the service time in other pewes, for the first time ij*d*., and the seconde time iiij*d*., to be emploied to the poores boxe ; provided eny, at the lessons and the sermons, the more better to heare may remove.

APPENDIX III.

List of Local and Obsolete Words found in these Churchwardens' Accounts.

allelmas, 30
amblettes, 80
anontes, 157, opposite
autor, 2, an altar
baudrick, 4
bost, 51
brastes, 80
burelle, 85
callends, callans, 108 et passim
cantylcope, 24
cather, 129
clammes, 29, iron clamps
clystes, 84
crule, 2, a fine worsted thread
dandrick, 152
ellorns, 9, elder-trees
engle, 3
fat, 5
fylle, 62
gist, 104
gresle, 137
grate, 17, a trellis
grest, 115
gudgeon, 62, 67
heche nails, 151
houle nails, 91
houslinge people, 82
howpe, 90, see whop
incle, 3; inkille, 26, a coarse
    sort of tape
klyfft, 110
kreking, 136
lade-payle, 87
lasp, 13, a latch
leste, 104
leystall, 5
licor, 90

loitore, 11
maylinge coordes, 35
paralynge, 62
prise, (parvise) 104
peise, 11, 105, weight
penting, 33, 56
pit, 4
porrelz, 58
pydelusse, 89
ramelle, 10, 46, rubbish
rasters, 118
ring, 11, 35, 125, a measure
runge, 161, the same as ring
seam, 23, a horse-load ; sheme,
    34, 39, 109
shoting, shuting, shotting, 30, 33
skallens, see callends.
skynes, 119
slore, 81
staffpes, 126
stoke, 30, a measure
stokynge, 65
storringe, 119
strick, 165, a measure
thele, 110
tilestones, 161
tonaculle, 56
tryssille, 90
walker, 141, a fuller
weyche, 10
whop, 35, 69, a measure; see
    howpe
whyrle-gate, 44
wont, 164, 165, a mole
wynding, 42
yat, 15, a gate.

INDEX.

INDEX OF NAMES.

www.ingramcontent.com/pod-product-compliance
Lightning Source LLC
Chambersburg PA
CBHW030837270326
41928CB00007B/1097